Abingdon's

Bible ZONE ®

Where the Bible Comes to Life

Younger Elementary 6

Celebrate Jesus

Also available from Abingdon Press:

Abingdon's BibleZone™
Preschool 6
Teacher's Guide

Abingdon's BibleZone™
Preschool 6
FUNspirational™ Kit

Abingdon's BibleZone™
Younger Elementary 6
FUNspirational™ Kit

Abingdon's BibleZone™
Older Elementary 6
Teacher's Guide

Abingdon's BibleZone™
Older Elementary 6
FUNspirational™ Kit

Writer/Editor: LeeDell Stickler
Bible stories: Sharilyn S. Adair
Production Editor: Lucinda Anderson
Production and Design Manager:
R. E. Osborne
Designer: Paige Easter
Cover Photo: Sid Dorris
Illustrator: Megan Jeffery

Abingdon's

Bible ZONE

®

Younger Elementary

6

Where the Bible Comes to Life

CELEBRATE JESUS

Abingdon Press
Nashville

Table of Contents

Celebrate Jesus

5

Bible Units in the Zone™

For those persons who wish to organize the stories in BibleZone™ as short term elective studies, here is a suggested plan.

1

The Whole World Celebrates Jesus

1. The Angel's Message — You will bear a Son, and you will name him Jesus. Luke 1:31

2. Joseph's Dream — Mary will bear a son, and you are to name him Jesus. Matthew 1:21, adapted

3. Jesus Is Born! — Mary gave birth to her first born son and wrapped him in bands of cloth, and laid him in a manger. Luke 2:7, adapted

4. Shepherds Kept Watch — To you is born this day in the city of David a Savior, who is the Messiah, the Lord. Luke 2:11

5. Simeon and Anna — Lord, you have kept your promise. Luke 2:29, *Good News Bible*

6. Follow That Star! — When they saw that the star had stopped, they were overwhelmed with joy. Matthew 2:10

2

Jesus' Teachings

7. Talking to God — Lord, teach us to pray. Luke 11:1

8. A Beattitude Attitude — Be happy and glad, for a great reward is kept for you in heaven. Matthew 5:9

9. The Great Commandment — Love the Lord your God with all your heart love your neighbor as yourself. Matthew 22:37–39, adapted

10. Forgive — Forgive one another. Ephesians 4:32, *Good News Bible*

11. The Least of These — Let us love, not in word or speech, but in truth and action. 1 John 3:18

12. Birds of the Field — Leave all your worries with God, because God cares for you. 1 Peter 5:7, adapted

13. The Golden Rule — Do for others what you want them to do for you. Matthew 7:12

About Bible ZONE

ZoneZillies™:

ZoneZillies™ are game and storytelling props found in the BibleZone™ FUNspirational™ Kit. Some ZoneZillies™ are consumable and will need to be replaced. These are added for the teacher's convenience.

- inflatable bell
- jewel light
- gold shred
- prism bag
- lion and lamb puppets
- kazoos
- laser disk shooter
- foam dice

- comet ball
- jewel balls
- tinsel wig
- metallic streamers
- pompoms
- friction cars
- Cassette with music by Brentwood Kids Music

Supplies:

- Bible
- construction paper
- two AA batteries (jewel light)
- plastic resealable bags
- cleaning supplies
- food coloring
- muslin (one yard per child)
- masking tape, clear tape
- index cards
- pencils
- dried grass, pebbles, sand
- six-inch thin paper plates
- posterboard
- hoola hoop
- shoeboxes
- fabric scraps
- bandannas or scarfs
- string or yarn
- cotton balls, cotton swabs
- yardstick or pointer

- tea or votive candles
- paper punch
- glass jars
- biblical costumes
- baby doll, blankets
- flashlights
- yellow or gold ribbon
- artificial flowers, feathers, faux jewels
- wooden paint stirrers (optional)
- stapler, staples
- facial or bathroom tissue
- glitter (optional)
- white glue
- plastic dish pans
- basket
- spray adhesive
- googly eyes (optional)
- recycled newspaper
- towels

Where the Bible Comes to Life

Have fun as the children learn about Jesus' birth and Jesus' teachings in Celebrate Jesus. Each lesson in this teacher guide is filled with games and activities that will make learning FUN-spirational™ for you and your children. With just a few added supplies, everything you need to teach is included in the Abingdon's BibleZone™ FUNspirational™ Kit. Games and activities encourage the children to play together and learn together.

Each lesson has a ZoneIn™ box:

> **We can celebrate God's gift of Jesus.**

that is repeated over and over again throughout the lesson. The ZoneIn™ states the Bible message in words your children will understand.

Use the following tips to help make your trip into the BibleZone™ a FUNspirational™ success!
- Read through each lesson. Read the Bible passages.
- Memorize the Bible verse and the ZoneIn™ statement.
- Choose what activities fit your unique group of children and your time limitations.
- Practice telling the BibleZone™ story.
- Gather the ZoneZillies™ you will use for the lesson.
- Gather supplies (paper, glue, crayons, and so forth) that you will use for the lesson.
- Learn the music for the lesson from the BibleZone™ FUNspirational™ Cassette.
- Arrange your room space to fit the lesson. Move tables and chairs so there is plenty of room for the children to move around and to sit on the floor.
- Copy the Reproducible pages for the lesson.
- Copy the HomeZone™ page for parents.

Younger Elementary

Each child in your class is a one-of-a-kind child of God. Each child has his or her own name, background, family situation, and set of experiences. It is important to remember and celebrate the uniqueness of each child. Yet these one-of-a-kind children of God have some common needs.

- All children need love.
- All children need a sense of self-worth.
- All children need to feel a sense of accomplishment.
- All children need to have a safe place to be and to express their feelings.
- All children need to be surrounded by adults who love them.
- All children need to experience the love of God.

Younger elementary (children ages 6-8 years old) also have some common characteristics.

Their Bodies

- They are growing at different rates.
- They are energetic, restless, and have difficulty sitting still.
- They are developing fine motor skills.
- They want to participate rather than watch or listen.

Their Minds

- They are developing basic academic skills.
- They are eager to learn new things.
- They learn best by working imaginatively and creatively.
- They have little sense of time.
- They are concrete thinkers and cannot interpret symbols.
- They are developing an ability to reason and discuss.
- They like to have a part in planning their own activities.

Their Relationships

- They want to play with other children.
- They are sensitive about the feelings of others.
- They are shifting their dependence from parents to teachers.
- They enjoy team activities but often dispute the rules.
- They imitate adults in attitudes and actions.

Their Hearts

- They are open to learning about God.
- They need caring adults who model Christian behaviors.
- They need to sing, move to, and say Bible verses.
- They need to hear simple Bible stories.
- They can talk with God easily if encouraged.
- They are beginning to ask questions about God.
- They can share with others.

The Angel's Message

Enter the **Zone**™

Bible Verse

You will bear a Son, and you will name him Jesus.

Luke 1:31

Bible Story
Luke 1:26-38

Mary was engaged, or betrothed, to Joseph when the angel appeared to her. Betrothals in Jewish tradition were usually arranged when girls were quite young and were as legally binding as marriage. Unlike a modern engagement, a betrothal could be broken only by divorce. Both Matthew and Luke state that Jesus was conceived by the Holy Spirit, without an act by a human father. We call this the virgin birth. It is important to remember that it is the activity and power of the Holy Spirit in the birth of Jesus that is emphasized, not the lack of a human father. The virgin birth is hardly mentioned elsewhere in the New Testament. There are no references that make the deity of Christ stand or fall by the method of his birth.

The word *angel* means "messenger." The angel's message to Mary that day was the surprising news that Mary had been chosen to be the mother of the Son of God. While she first reacted with doubt and fear, her ultimate response was one of obedience and faith. Even though she knew her life was about to be unexpectedly changed, Mary trusted God.

We too are called to respond to God with the same kind of obedience and trust that Mary had. As a teacher of young children, you can provide a model that can influence the faith development of the children in your classroom. Younger elementary children are beginning to expand their exclusive dependence on their parents and relatives to include their teachers. This trust is influenced by their own life experiences. Your students will come from a variety of backgrounds and family situations. Some of the children may not be surrounded by adults who model trust and keep promises. You can be a safe and trustworthy adult; one who leads your children to a sense of trust in God.

We celebrate the coming of the Savior.

Scope the ZONE ™

ZONE	TIME	SUPPLIES	⊙ ZILLIES ™
Zoom Into the Zone			
Jesse's Jumble	5 minutes	Reproducible 1A, crayons or felt-tip markers	none
Jesse Tree Scramble	10 minutes	Reproducible 1B, masking tape	none
BibleZone ™			
Angel's Choice	10 minutes	none	medium-sized pom-pom, metallic wig
The Angel's Message	5 minutes	none	none
Christmas Count down	10 minutes	Reproducibles 1B and 6B, strips of red and green construction paper, white glue or tape, scissors	none
LifeZone			
Sing and Celebrate	10 minutes	flashlights, cassette player	Cassette
Gonna Have a Baby	5 minutes	none	inflatable bell
Ring Out the News	5 minutes	none	inflatable bell

⊙ Zillies ™ are found in the **BibleZone ™ FUNspirational ™ Kit.**

Choose one or more activities to catch your children's interest.

Supplies:
Reproducible 1A, crayons or felt-tip markers

Zillies™:
none

Jesse's Jumble

(G) reet the children as they enter the room. Hand out a copy of Jesse's Jumble *(Reproducible 1A)*.

Say: **We are going to talk about the many different ways people around the world celebrate Jesus' birthday. Many years ago in Europe, people set up a special tree for Christmas. It was called a Jesse Tree. On this tree the people would hang symbols of persons and stories from the Bible. The tree was named after Jesse, King David's father, because God had promised to send the people a Savior who would be related to King David. That's Jesse sitting at the base of the tree. Joseph was related to King David. See how many Bible stories you can find.**

Display the Jesse tree symbols *(Reproducible 1B)* to help the children identify the hidden pictures. Let the children try to identify the various Bible stories the pictures suggest: (Adam and Eve—apple, snake; Noah and the flood—ark, rainbow; Joseph—coat of many colors; Moses—clay tablets; Jonah—whale; prophets—scroll; David—shepherd's crook, star; Jesus—cross, lily, dove; Ruth—wheat; hammer—Joseph.)

Supplies:
Reproducible 1B, masking tape

Zillies™:
none

Jesse Tree Scramble

(C) ut apart the Jesse Tree symbols. Put a loop of masking tape on the back of each. Attach one symbol to each child. Have the children pull their chairs into a circle. Select one child to be IT. IT will stand in the center. Remove his or her chair from the circle.

Say: **IT is going to decorate his or her Jesse Tree. IT will call out the objects to hang on the tree. If you are wearing a picture of that object, then you will come to the center. When IT announces, "The Savior has come!" then all the ornaments will rush back to their places in the circle. IT will try to get one of the empty places. Whoever is left without a seat becomes the next IT.**

ZONE IN™ | **We celebrate the coming of the Savior.**

Bible Z❂NE™

Choose one or more activities to immerse your children in the Bible story.

Angel's Choice

(H)ave the children sit in the chairs and hold their hands in front of them on their laps. They should cup their two hands together.

Say: In Bible times the people had heard for many years that God was going to send a Savior. The people waited and waited and waited and waited. Sometimes they grew discouraged. But one day something happened. An angel came to the town of Nazareth and chose a young girl for a very special job. Let's play a game. One of you will be the angel. (Hand the metallic wig to one of the children.) The angel has a special message for one of the people in this circle. (*Hold up the pompom.*) Let's see if we can guess who the angel will choose.

Place the pom-pom in the palm of the angel. Show the angel how to hold his or her hands as though praying. This will sandwich the pom-pom between the angel's palms.

Say: Our angel will go around the circle and pass his or her hands through each of your open hands. Somewhere around the circle the angel will pass the special message to one of you. Let's see if we can guess who the angel chooses. Whoever guesses correctly gets to be the next angel.

Supplies:
none

Zillies:
medium-sized pom-pom, metallic wig

ZONE IN™ **We celebrate the coming of the Savior.**

Say: Children in many parts of the world play a game similar to this. In the country of Nigeria, the game is called Booko.

Ask: Do you think the people who were waiting for a Messiah ever wondered who it would be? How would you know? What sign would God send? Who would be the mother of this special person?

Say: Perhaps girls like Mary even daydreamed that they would be the one that God would choose.

The Angel's Message

by Sharilyn S. Adair

Say: You are going to help me tell the Bible story today. There are actions that you will do with me and some you will do when you hear these words:

Angel - stand tall and raise both arms above the head. Bring arms down as though flapping large wings.

Mary - Place both palms together as though praying and bring them to the chest while bowing the head.

Baby - Place one hand on top of the other, palms up, and rock the arms back and forth as though rocking a baby.

Jesus - Make the American Sign Language sign for Jesus: Place the middle finger of the right hand in the center of the left palm and then immediately switch hands and place the middle finger of the left hand in the center of the right palm.

Sweep. Sweep. Sweep. (*Make sweeping motions.*) **Mary** swept the broom across the hard dirt floor. As she swept she sang a little song. (*Sing a little song.*) **Mary** was excited but she wasn't exactly sure why. Perhaps she would see Joseph today. (*Sigh deeply.*)

Joseph was the man that **Mary** was engaged to marry. He was a carpenter in the village of Nazareth. (*Pound fist into palm of opposite hand. Then pretend to saw.*) **Mary** would be proud when she was the town carpenter's wife. (*Hold head high and puff out chest.*)

Sweep, sweep, sweep. The straw bristles left little furrows in the dirt.

(*Pretend to sweep.*) Sunlight streamed through the windows. (*Hold hand to forehead as though shielding the eyes.*) But no, it was too bright for sunlight! Much too bright! Besides, there was now another person in the room with **Mary.** (*Look startled. Shout "eek!"*)

"Don't be afraid, **Mary**," said an unfamiliar voice, "for you have found favor with God."

But **Mary** could not help being a little frightened. How many people living in a small clay house in a little village are visited by **angels?** Not many, **Mary** was sure. But here was one, standing as big as life in her house. And the **angel** seemed perfectly at home.

14

The **angel** stood in the center of the room. The light that surrounded him filled every corner.

Mary became braver and took two steps forward. Then she spoke, "Who are you and what do you want with me?"

The **angel** smiled. "I have come with a special message for you. A message from God. You are going to have a **baby**. The **baby** will be a son, and you are to name him **Jesus.**"

"How can I have a **baby**?" asked Mary. (*Scratch head as though wondering.*) "Joseph and I are not yet married."

The **angel** answered, "Nothing is impossible with God. **Jesus** will be a special child. He will be God's son. He will save his people."

Then **Mary** said to the **angel**, "I will do whatever God wants me to do. I am God's servant," and she bowed her head. When she looked up again, the **angel** was gone.

Oh my, thought **Mary**. I must tell Joseph the good news.

Thank you, God, for Jesus.

Bible Zone™

Supplies:
Reproducibles 1B and 6B, strips of red and green construction paper, white glue or tape, scissors

Zillies™:
none

Christmas Countdown

Say: The people in Bible times waited a long, long time for God to send a Savior. Surely sometimes they must have gotten discouraged and thought that God had forgotten them. But they reminded themselves that God promised and God always keeps promises.

Ask: What are some things you do as you wait for Christmas? (*Invite the children to share some of their own family traditions.*) How many of you have an Advent calendar? (*Allow the children who have used one to explain how it works. You might want to bring one in to show the class.*)

Say: The Advent calendar is a special tradition that came to us from Europe. Today people all over the world have special ways of counting down the days until Jesus' birthday. We call this special time of waiting and getting ready Advent. Let's make a Christmas Countdown to use during Advent.

Give each child a copy of the Advent Star *(Reproducible 6B)* and the Advent Chain links *(Reproducible 1B)*. Let the children cut out the links. Alternate a red strip of construction paper and a white piece of construction paper until all the white activity strips have been used and there are twenty-five links. (Or you may want to determine how many days are in Advent, since this number varies from year to year. Advent begins on the fourth Sunday before Christmas.)

Say: Hang this chain in your bedroom. Each day unhook one of the links. When you unhook a white link, do the activity listed there.

We celebrate the coming of the Savior.

16

Choose one or more activities to bring the Bible to life.

Sing and Celebrate

Bring the children together in an open area of the room.

Say: In the country of Nigeria in Africa, Christmas comes at the hottest time of the year. Imagine having Christmas in the summer. In the northeastern part of Nigeria is a group of people known as the Wurkum people. The day before Christmas is when the Christians who own lanterns form a group and sing carols from dark until Christmas morning. On Christmas day there are no gifts exchanged. The people have a short worship service and then the whole village goes about the countryside singing and telling the Christmas story to everyone they meet.

Plan a parade. Let the children bring flashlights for lanterns. Parade through the halls of the church singing this song. As the children come across persons in the hall or other classes, let them tell the Christmas story in their own words and sing a carol.

An African Nativity
(Sing Noel)

REFRAIN:
Sing Noel, Sing Noel, Noel, Noel
Sing Noel, Sing Noel, Noel, Noel,
Sing Noel, Sing Noel, Noel, Noel,
Sing Noel, Sing Noel, Noel, Noel,

Sing we all Noel. Sing we all Noel.
Sing we all Noel. Sing we all Noel.
Sing we all Noel. Sing we all Noel.
Sing we all Noel. Sing we all Noel.

REFRAIN:
Sing Noel, Sing Noel, Noel, Noel
Sing Noel, Sing Noel, Noel, Noel,
Sing Noel, Sing Noel, Noel, Noel,
Sing Noel, Sing Noel, Noel, Noel,
Sing. Sing. Sing. Sing. Sing.

Arranged by Dave Williamson

Supplies:
flashlights, cassette player

Zillies™:
Cassette

♣ Noel means an exclamation of joy.

Life Zone™

Choose one or more activities to bring the Bible to life.

Supplies:
none

Zillies™:
inflatable bell

Gonna Have a Baby

Teach the children the following response:

Response:
Going to have a baby.
Going to name him Jesus.
And peace will fill the world.

Say: I will read some phrases and when I come to the question at the end, I will throw the bell to someone in the circle. Whoever catches the bell will have to say the response.

After each four-line rhyme, pitch the bell to someone in the circle.

When Mary was at home
In Nazareth one day,
An angel came to see her.
What did the angel say?

Joseph was a carpenter
He hammered wood all day.
The angel came to visit him.
What did the angel say?

"You are blessed," the angel said.
"The Lord will find a way."
"I'm not afraid," said Mary.
"Let it be just as you say."

For all the earth God had a plan
That would come about one day.
It all began with a girl named Mary,
Who heard an angel say:

Supplies:
none

Zillies™:
inflatable bell

Ring Out the News

Hold up the inflatable bell as you ask: "What's the good news?"

Toss the bell to one of the children. Have him or her respond with good news. For example, "Jesus is coming!"; "Jesus is born!"; or "God sent Jesus!" Then, that child will ask the same question and pass the bell to another child in the circle. When the bell has made it to every child in the circle, have the children form a prayer circle.

Pray: Dear God, as we celebrate the days before Christmas, help us to remember your most special gift, Jesus, the Savior. Amen.

Have all the children put their hands in the center on top of yours as you **ask: What's the good news?** (*Have the children count down: one, two, three, and answer "Jesus is born!"*)

Make a copy of HomeZone™ for each family in your class.

Bible Verse
You will bear a Son, and you will name him Jesus.
Luke 1:31

Bible Story
Luke 1:26-38

In today's lesson your child heard about the angel's message to Mary. She was about to be the mother of God's only son Jesus. What a life-changing event for a young girl! To deal with this change of plans, Mary had to be willing to put her complete trust in God. In a time where more and more people feel that they only have themselves and a few select persons they can count on, perhaps the hardest thing for a child is extending trust to someone she or he cannot see. Help your child understand that God is always there. God promised to send a Savior, a Messiah. And Jesus was this long-awaited person.

Make an Advent Calendar

Let's count down to Christmas using a European tradition—an Advent Calendar. Advent calendars come in a variety of forms. Ours will be a Christmas tree.

You will need: green construction paper, scissors, tape, and individually wrapped pieces of candy.

Advent begins on the fourth Sunday before Christmas. It does not always begin on the first day of December. To determine how many pieces of candy you will need for your tree, begin with Christmas Day. Count backward four Sundays. The fourth Sunday will be the first Sunday in Advent. Now, count the days until Christmas. You will need a corresponding number of candies for the tree.

Cut a Christmas tree shape from the construction paper. Attach the candies with invisible tape. Each day remove one piece of candy. When Christmas arrives, the tree will be undecorated. Make sure it is large enough to attach the candies. For Advent you will need one piece of candy for each day.

Zone In

We celebrate the coming of the Savior.

Reproducible 1A

BIBLEZONE™

Wish someone a Merry Christmas.

Sing your favorite Christmas carol.

Read Luke 2:1-20.

Make and send a Christmas card to someone.

Visit someone who needs cheering up.

Thank God for five things.

Give someone a hug.

Make gift tags from old Christmas cards.

Reproducible 1B

Joseph's Dream

Enter the ZONE™

Bible Verse

Mary will bear a son, and you are to name him Jesus.

Matthew 1:21, adapted

Bible Story
Matthew 1:18–25

In the Old Testament of the Bible, God promised King David that David's descendants would sit on the throne of Israel forever. But the little country that David ruled did not stay independent for long. The people, however, always relied on God's promise and looked for God to provide a king, like David, who would restore Israel to her former greatness. The story of Jesus' birth in the Gospels presents Jesus as this promised one—the fulfillment of God's promise through the ages.

The angel who visits Joseph in a dream reminds him of the promise of the Messiah, found in Isaiah. Isaiah tells us the qualities of the ideal king and promises that the king will come from the line of Jesse, King David's father. The angel even refers to Joseph as "son of David," calling to mind Joseph's lineage. Joseph is of David's ancestral line, a crucial element in the fulfillment of God's promise. In Matthew's account of Jesus' birth, part of the miracle, apart from the conception, is fitting Jesus into Joseph's family.

The importance of Joseph's role is further stressed in the naming of the baby. In those times it was common for the mother to name the baby. But in this instance Joseph is to name the baby Jesus.

Children of this generation face a variety of concerns that are unfamiliar to many adults. In the midst of all the Christmas commercialism and societal woes, you can give your students a very important message: God is with us—regardless. Children may be worried about questions of whether they will be good enough to receive presents from Santa. Unlike the conditional promises of Santa, God promises love without condition. This is an important message for first- and second-graders and, indeed, it is an important message for all of us!

We celebrate God's gift of Jesus.

Scope the ZONE ™

ZONE	TIME	SUPPLIES	⊚ ZILLIES™
Zoom Into the Zone			
Angels on the Move	10 minutes	Reproducible 2A, string or yarn, white glue, crayons or felt-tip markers, glitter (optional), scissors	gold shred
Are You Sleeping?	10 minutes	none	none
BibleZone™			
Do the Opposite	5 minutes	none	none
In Your Dreams, Joseph	5 minutes	none	none
Let's Connect!	5 minutes	Reproducible 2B, scissors, (Option: construction paper, glue	none
LifeZone			
Sing and Celebrate	10 minutes	cassette player	Cassette
Heavenly Verses	7 minutes	Reproducible 2B, cassette player, felt-tip marker	Cassette
Ring Out the News	3 minutes	none	inflatable bell

⊚ Zillies™ are found in the **BibleZone™ FUNspirational™ Kit.**

Choose one or more activities to catch your children's interest.

Supplies:
Reproducible 2A, string or yarn, white glue, crayons or felt-tip markers, glitter (optional), scissors

Zillies:
gold shred

Angels on the Move

Set out the supplies the children will need for the angel mobile: two angel patterns *(Reproducible 1A)*, string or yarn, white glue, glitter (optional), **gold shred**, crayons or felt-tip markers.

Greet the children as they arrive. Try to say something personal to each child.

Say: Today we are going to hear a story about another angel's visit. This angel stopped Joseph from doing something he would regret.

Have the children cut out and decorate their angels. Then show them how to assemble the mobile. (See the illustration on this page.) Hang them in the room.

We celebrate God's gift of Jesus.

Supplies:
none

Zillies™:
none

Are You Sleeping?

Have the children form a line at one end of an open area. Place a chair at the other end of the area. This is where Joseph will sleep.

Say: In today's story Joseph hears some distressing news. The night after he hears Mary's news, God sends an angel to him in his sleep. Let's pretend that we are the angel. Let's see if we can sneak up on him and deliver the message. We'll call out, "Joseph, are you sleeping?" If he snores, then we can get a step closer. If he answers "No!" then we have to scramble back to the line. If Joseph catches one of us before we get back to the line, that person becomes Joseph.

Select one child to be Joseph. Joseph sits in the chair and responds to the question. Play the game until most of the children have had a chance to be Joseph.

Bible ZONE™

Choose one or more activities to immerse your children in the Bible story.

Do the Opposite

Bring the children together in a circle.

Say: In today's Bible story we will hear about Joseph and his part in the birth of God's son. Now, Joseph was a man of the community. He was a carpenter, an upstanding man. He followed all the rules and all the laws. Joseph took pride that he was an upstanding man of the village. But after his encounter with the angel, he found he had to do the opposite of what was expected, the opposite of what was the rule. He had to go against tradition.

Continue: Let's play a game of opposites. I want you to do the opposite of everything I say. Everyone stand up. Everyone sit down. Everyone face me. Everyone face the opposite wall. Stand on both feet. Stand on one foot. Turn to the left. Turn to the right. Stand very still. Wiggle all over. Stop.

Ask: Was it difficult to do the opposite of what I said? Did you have to think about it a little?

Say: Well, Joseph had to think about it, too. But in the end he did what God told him to do. Joseph played an important role in the birth of God's son. Joseph was related to King David.

ZONE IN™

We celebrate God's gift of Jesus.

Supplies:
none

Zillies™:

In Your Dreams, Joseph

by Sharilyn S. Adair

Ask: Have you ever been in a stadium or arena where people do a cheer called the wave? What does it look like? *(One at a time people stand up and sit down. From a distance this looks like a wave.)*

Say: Today we are going to tell the Bible story using the wave. I will either start an action or say a word. Then the person sitting on my right will do it, then the child on that person's right, then the next boy or girl, and so on until it gets back to me. Then I will continue the story.

Let the children practice doing the wave by clapping, standing up, and then saying, "Jesus loves me" in wave fashion. Then begin the story.

Joseph was asleep.

Wave action: Snore.

It was a worried sleep.

Wave action: Snore.

He tossed and turned.

Wave action: Put folded hands under left cheek and turn to left.

He turned and tossed.

Wave action: Put folded hands under right cheek and turn to right.

Joseph was engaged to Mary, a young girl in the village.

Wave action: Hold out left hand as though showing off an engagement ring.

But they weren't married yet.

Wave action: Draw left hand back into the body.

And Joseph wasn't sure they would be.

Wave action: "Harrumph!"

Mary was going to have a baby.

Wave action: Pretend to rock baby.

She said the baby was God's son.

Wave action: Rock the baby.

Joseph didn't know what to do.

Wave action: Shrug shoulders and hold up hands.

As Joseph slept he heard a voice.

Wave action: Hold hands to mouth, turn to person on the right and say, "Psst."

"Who is it?" asked Joseph.

Wave action: Whisper "Who is it?"

"I'm an angel from God," said the voice.

Wave action: Turn to person on right and say, "an angel!"

"Am I dreaming?" asked Joseph

Wave action: Snore.

"Yes, but pay attention anyway," said the angel.

Wave action: Turn to person on right and pat her or him on the head.

"Don't be afraid to take Mary for your wife."

Wave action:

"Her son is very special."

Wave action: Stand up and say "special" then sit down.

"You shall name him Jesus."

Wave action: Say "Jesus".

"He will save his people from their sins."

Wave action: Stand up, raise arms overhead, and say "Yay!"

Then the angel went away.

Wave action: Wave goodbye.

And Joseph slept peacefully the rest of the night..

Wave action: Snore.

The next day Joseph knew just what to do.

Wave action: Stomp foot decisively.

Joseph would marry Mary. He would help her take care of Jesus..

Wave action: Rock the baby.

The end.

Wave action: Say "the end."

Bible Zone™

Choose one or more activities to immerse your children in the Bible story.

Supplies:
Reproducible 2B, scissors (Option: construction paper, glue)

Zillies™:
none

Let's Connect!

Divide the children into teams of three or four children. If you have a small class, simply let each child be a team. Give each team a set of the Christmas symbols. Let them cut the symbols apart and spread them on the table in front of them.

Say: When we celebrate Christmas, we use many things to help us remember the stories about Jesus. Let's see if you can figure out how each of these pictures connects with Christmas. I will talk about a particular picture. As soon as you recognize it, pick it up and wave it high in the air. The first team to wave will receive a point.

1. This stands for Jesus Christ, the light of the world. (*candle*)
2. This messenger from God told Mary and Joseph the good news. (*angel*)
3. This reminds us to ring out the good news and tell everyone we know about Jesus. (*bell*)
4. This thorny evergreen reminds us that Jesus wore a crown of thorns. (*holly*)
5. This circle of evergreen hangs on the door to greet people and says, "Jesus gives eternal life." (*Christmas wreath*)
6. This led the way for the wise men to find the child Jesus. (*star*)
7. This sweet treat reminds us of the crook used by the shepherd's who were the first to hear the good news. (*candy cane*)
8. With a star at its top and lights on the branches, this reminds us that Christ is always with us. (*Christmas tree*)
9. We give these to one another because Jesus was God's special gift. These also remind us of the gold, frankincense, and myrrh that the wise men brought with them. (*presents*)
10. This is the way we sing praises to God and tell the story of the birth of Jesus. (*music*)
11. These sweet treats are ways we celebrate the goodness of our life because of God's gift. (*gingerbread cookie*)
12. This reminds us that God sent Jesus to live among us. (*baby in the manger*)

Note: If you want to let the children use these pictures as a game, make two copies for each game. Cut out and glue onto colored construction paper. Play the game as a game of concentration.

We can celebrate God's gift of Jesus.

Choose one or more activities to bring the Bible to life.

Sing and Celebrate

Supplies:
cassette player

Zillies™:
Cassette

(S)ay: In many parts of the world Christmas is not a time of snow and ice. It is a time of sunshine and warm weather. For example, if we went to the Caribbean, to the island of Jamaica, we wouldn't decorate with holly and mistletoe, but we might use palm branches, orchids, and seashells. Instead of coats and mittens at Christmas, we might wear shorts, sandals, and bathing suits. Let's learn a song that was written about Christmas in the style of the people of Jamaica.

The Virgin Mary Had a Baby Boy

De Virgin Mary had a baby boy:
De Virgin Mary had a baby boy:
De Virgin Mary had a baby boy:
They said that His name was Jesus.

De angels sang when de baby was born
De angels sang when de baby was born.
De angels sang when de baby was born.
They said that His name was Jesus.

REFRAIN:
He come from de glory,
He come from de glorious kingdom.
He come from de glory.
He come from de glorious kingdom.

REFRAIN (Repeat)

Arranged by Dave Williamson

Life Zone™

Choose one or more activities to bring the Bible to life.

Supplies:
Reproducible 2B,
cassette player,
felt-tip marker

Zillies™:
Cassette

Heavenly Verses

Make twelve copies of the angel *(Reproducible 2B.)* Write one word of the Bible verse (See page 22.) on each angel. Arrange the angels in a circle. If you have more than twelve children, make blank angels and place them around the circle, as well.

Have each child stand on an angel. Play "The Virgin Mary Had a Baby Boy" from the **cassette**. Let the children march around the circle. After a few moments stop the music. When the music stops, each child must pick up the angel that he or she is standing on and get in the order of the Bible verse. Time the children. Then place the angels on the floor and do the activity again.

We can celebrate God's gift of Jesus.

Supplies:
none

Zillies™:
inflatable bell

Ring Out the News!

Have the children form a prayer circle. Hold the **bell** out in front and let each child place his or her hands on the bell. This might mean that you have a very tight circle if you have a large group.

When everyone is touching the **bell**, **pray: Dear God, we thank you for your gift of Jesus. Help us to remember Jesus in everything we do as we prepare to celebrate his birthday. Amen.**

Ask: What's the good news? (*Jesus is born!*) **What did you say?** (*Jesus is born!*) **I still can't hear you!** (*Jesus is born!*)

On the third response, toss the **bell** up into the air, and let everyone cheer.

Make a copy of HomeZone™ for each family in the class.

Bible Verse
Mary will bear a son, and you are to name him Jesus.
Matthew 1:21, adapted

Bible Story
Matthew 1:18–25

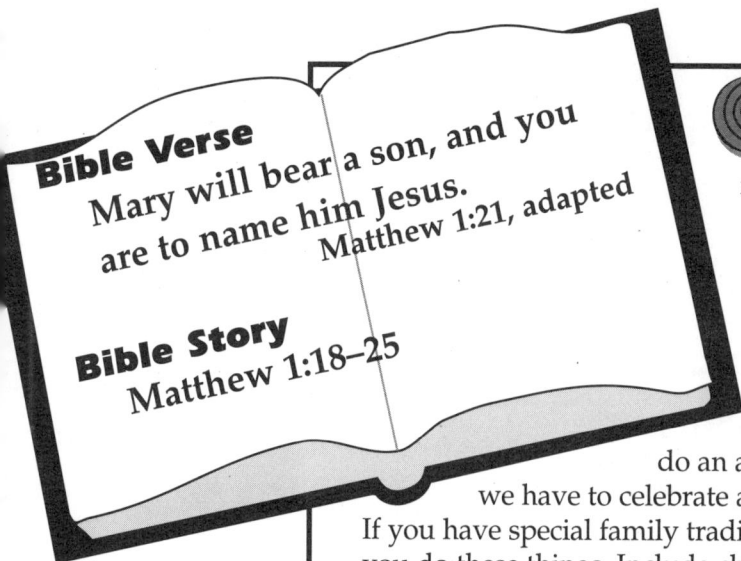

In today's Bible story your child heard about the angel's message to Joseph. At first when Joseph heard the news that Mary was expecting a baby, he was not too excited. In fact, his first plans were to quietly divorce Mary so as not to cause a scandal. Actually he was being very charitable, since a pregnancy at this stage usually signified adultery, punishable by stoning. But God's messenger made Joseph do an about-face. As we celebrate the birth of Jesus we have to celebrate all the people who were a part of Jesus' life. If you have special family traditions, explain to your child or children why you do these things. Include children in creating new traditions that they can pass to their own children.

Deck the Halls

Most countries celebrate Christmas. But each country has developed its own special traditions, stories, and decorations. The Christmas tree in all its various forms has become a centerpiece for the Christian Christmas. On the tree families hang ornaments that represent many different events and memories. A good family project would be to make Finnish Cornucopias to hang on the tree and hand out to visitors as they come to visit during the holidays.

Supplies: heavy foil Christmas wrap, glue or tape, metallic chenille sticks, scissors, six-inch paper plate (pattern), pencil, individual candy treats.

1. Draw around the pattern on the foil paper. Cut out the circle. Fold the circle in half. Cut along the folded line.
2. Form a cone-shaped basket from the semi-circle. Glue or tape the edges together.
3. Make a handle from a chenille stick or cut a paper strip and glue for the handle.
4. Fill each cornucopia with candies and hang on the tree.

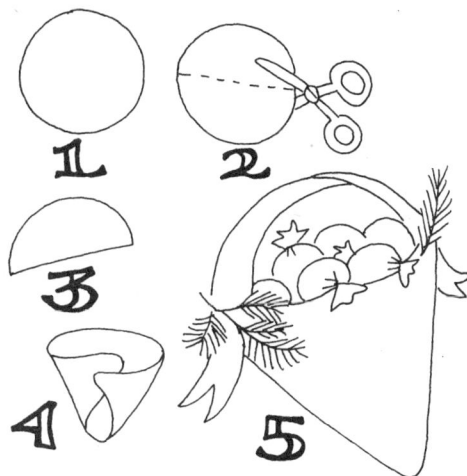

Zone IN

We can celebrate God's gift of Jesus.

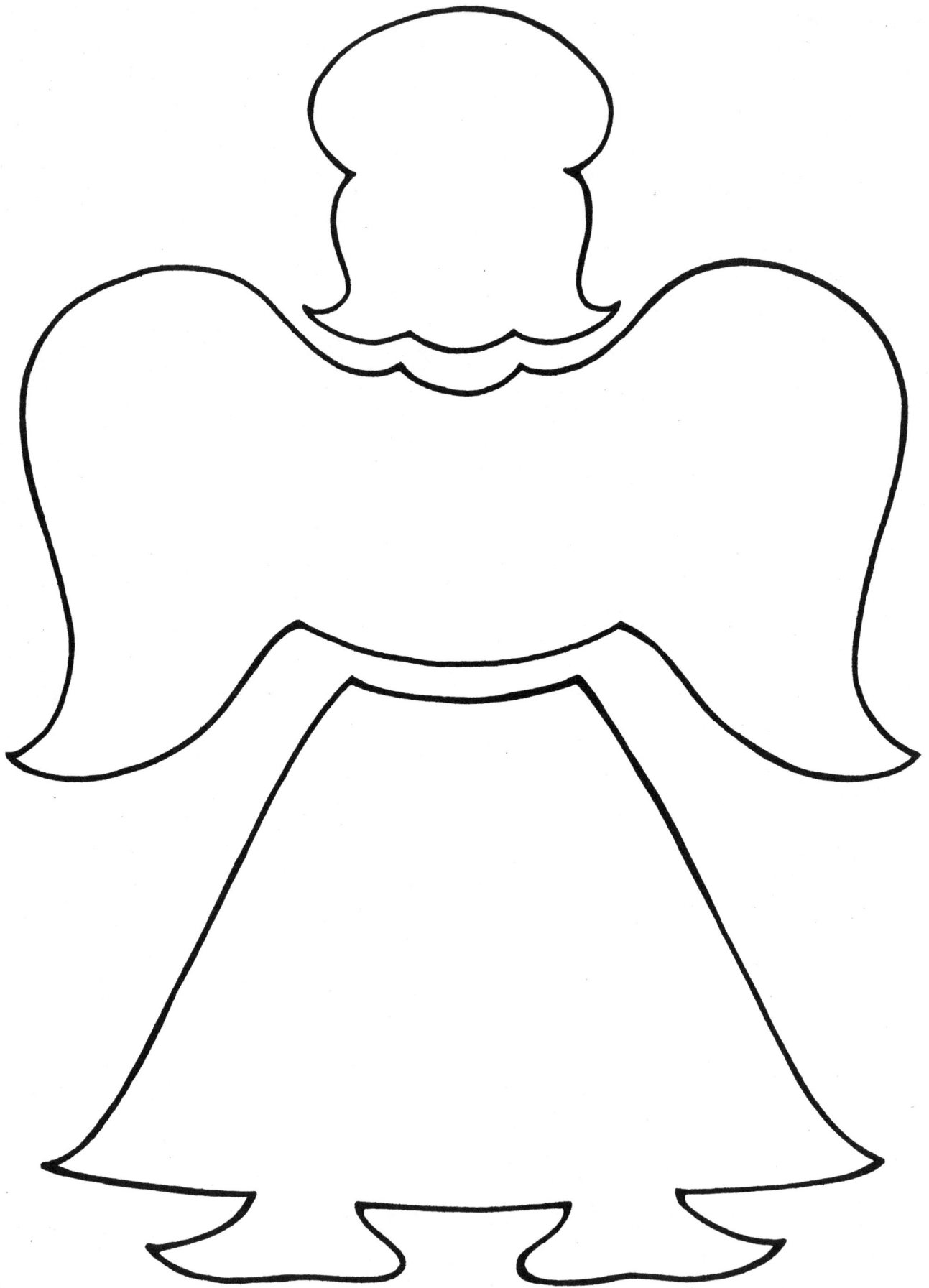

Reproducible 2A

BibleZone™

Reproducible 2B

Permission granted to photocopy for local church use. © 1998 Abingdon Press.

Jesus Is Born!

Enter the ZONE™

Bible Verse
Mary gave birth to her firstborn son and wrapped him in bands of cloth, and laid him in a manger.

Luke 2:7, adapted

Bible Story
Luke 2:1-7

Caesar Augustus, the emperor of Rome, had ordered a census of the people under his rule. With the idea of raising more tax money, enrollment required that a man appear for census in the city from which his ancestors came. Since Joseph was part of the house of David, Mary and Joseph had to travel from Nazareth to Bethlehem. This was about a ninety-mile journey and would have been difficult under any circumstance, but particularly for a man and his pregnant wife.

Bethlehem was on a main caravan route. Caravans often stopped there to replenish food and water. Individual travelers, however, usually depended on the hospitality of the townspeople. Strangers could expect to be welcomed in people's homes as they traveled and for the time that the travelers stayed, they were considered part of the family. Because of the crowded conditions in Bethlehem, Mary and Joseph were unable to find a place to stay, either in a private home or in a guesthouse or inn.

The accommodations the young couple found were humble but adequate. And when the time came for Mary to give birth, she carried on just as her mother had done before her. She washed her baby's body and rubbed him with salt. Then she wrapped him in bands of soft cloth. These bands kept the baby warm and helped his body grow straight and strong. Then, Mary laid Baby Jesus in his cradle—a feed trough for the animals of the inn.

Few people would expect a king to be born in a stable to a poor family. Yet Jesus is the King of Kings. The unexpected circumstances of Jesus' birth remind us of the unexpectedness of God's action in our lives. In ways that we do not seek and in places that we do not expect, we can encounter the presence of God.

Christmas can be a particularly busy and stressful time of the year for most families. But many children are also experiencing the pressures of difficult family situations. Be sensitive to different family situations and to children who show that they are under pressure. Remember that God came down to us, in the midst of everything. Take time to celebrate the peace and the quiet as well.

We can celebrate the birth of Jesus.

Scope the ZONE™

ZONE	TIME	SUPPLIES	⊚ ZILLIES™
Zoom Into the Zone			
Make Animalitoes	15 minutes	Reproducible 3A, cotton balls or facial tissue, crayons or felt-tip markers, scissors, stapler, staples, yarn scraps, pencils, crayons, or felt-tip markers	none
BibleZone™			
Going to Bethlehem	10 minutes	chairs, open space, cassette player	jewel light, Cassette
The Peaceful Kingdom	10 minutes	baby doll and blankets, biblical costumes, ears for donkey, horns for cow, beak for dove, table for stage	lamb and lion puppets
What's in the Stable	5 minutes	blindfold	none
Hip Hop Hop	10 minutes	Reproducible 3B, scissors, masking tape	foam dice
LifeZone			
Sing and Celebrate	5 minutes	cassette player	Cassette
St. Lucia's Scramble	5 minutes	masking tape, open space	none
Ring Out the News	5 minutes	none	inflatable bell

⊚ Zillies™ are found in the **BibleZone™ FUNspirational™ Kit.**

Zoom Into the ZONE™

Choose one or more activities to catch your children's interest.

Reproducible 3A,
cotton balls or
facial tissue, sta-
pler, staples,
yarn scraps,
pencils, crayons
or felt-tip
markers

Zillies™:

Make Animalitoes

Make two copies of the *animalitoes* for each child in your group.

Greet the children as they come in. Direct them to tables where the supplies have been laid out. Get them started making their *animalitoes*.

Say: Christmas is a holiday that people all over the world celebrate. Each country celebrates in a different way. Today we are going to make a special decoration. The expert weavers of Guatemala make these *animalitoes* **(animal EE toes), or little animals, from hand-woven cotton fabric. The** *animalitoes* **are shaped like dogs, donkeys, sheep, elephants, bulls, and rabbits. But today, since we are going to hear a story about the trip to Bethlehem, our** *animalitoes* **will look like sheep or donkeys.** *(If you have a globe, show the children where Guatemala is.)*

Ask: What does a donkey have to do with a trip to Bethlehem? *(Invite the children to share the donkey's role.)* **How does the sheep relate to the Christmas story?** *(Shepherds heard the news of Jesus' birth first.)*

Have the children cut out the two sides of the animal each chooses to make. Place the two sides so that their noses face each other. Then let the children decorate the outsides of their animals with stripes, squiggles, or other designs. Have them make both animal pieces the same. Add dark, round eyes to both pieces. Once the outside is decorated, let the children create a tail and mane from the yarn scraps. Glue to the inside of one of the halves. With the crayon side out, staple the two pieces together around the bottom half. At the opening, stuff the animal with cotton balls or facial tissue. When sufficiently stuffed, staple closed. Tie a length of yarn around the donkeys neck. Form a loop to hang on the Christmas tree.

Option: If you have a longer time, the children may make their animalitoes out of cotton fabric. Instead of stapling around the edges, let the children stitch around the edges with a needle and thread.

We can celebrate the birth of Jesus.

Bible Z⊙NE™

Choose one or more activities to immerse your children in the Bible story.

Going to Bethlehem

Have the children bring chairs to an open area. Select one child to begin the game as IT. Have the rest of the children arrange their chairs in a line, side by side. Then turn every other chair in the opposite direction. There should be one less chair than the number of children present.

Give IT the **jewel light.** IT starts walking around the line of chairs in which the players are seated. IT says, "I am going to Bethlehem. I am going to Bethlehem!" IT stops now and then to tap the jewel light on the knees of a child. This is the signal for the one seated in the chair to get up and follow IT. The next one tapped must follow behind that player and so on until all the children are marching around the chairs in a single line with IT at the head. IT may even change directions. All the players must follow. While IT is marching around, the teacher will be playing a song from the **Cassette**. When the music stops, the players, including IT, make a scramble for the chairs. The player who is left without a chair is lost and is out of the game. The player who is out takes a chair from the end of the line and carries it to the sidelines. The player who was sitting on it becomes the next IT. Continue until there are two players and one chair left.

Say: It was fun playing "I'm Going to Bethlehem." In today's story Mary and Joseph have to make a trip from Nazareth to Bethlehem. This trip would take three whole days of traveling. I wonder if it was as much fun for Mary and Joseph as our pretend trip.

Ask: How did they have to travel? (*by foot and donkey*) **What did they have to take with them?** (*food and water and clothing*) **Where would they sleep?** (*wherever they could*) **Do you think you would have liked to travel in Bible times?**

ZONE IN™

We can celebrate the birth of Jesus.

Supplies:
chairs, open space, cassette player

Zillies™:
jewel light, Cassette

The Peaceful Kingdom

by LeeDell Stickler

The Christmas story is one that is so familiar to children because they hear it every year. Every year we tell the same story but in a slightly different way. Today the children are going to act out the story from a slightly different perspective. We will begin with the prophecy from the book of Isaiah.

You will need these characters: Narrator, Lamb, Lion, Mary, Joseph, innkeeper, donkey, dove, cow.

You will need these props: doll wrapped in swaddling clothes, biblical costumes, ears for donkey, horns for cow, beak for dove, table turned on its side for puppet stage.

Select the most confident readers for the parts of the narrator, the lamb, and the lion, since their dialogue is more extensive than the others. Make a copy of the play for each child. If you have a large class, let the children take turns presenting the play.

Lamb (*Snoring loudly*): Mmmph

Lion: Growl! Growl! (*ferociously*)

Sheep: Eeek! Eeek! A lion! I'm lamb chops!

Lion: I certainly hope you're tender. I'm mighty hungry today.

Narrator: Hold on! Hold on! Stop! (*Narrator stands between the two.*) You can't do this!

Lion: And just why not?

Sheep: (*Confused.*) Yeah, why not?

Narrator: The time has come. I know. I read about it in the Bible.

Lion: What's the Bible got to do with my dinner?

Lamb: Don't interrupt. Keep going.

Narrator: In the Bible we hear that the prophet Isaiah promised us that God would send a Savior. A child would be born. A son. And this child would be called "Wonderful Counselor," "Mighty God," "Eternal Father," and "Prince of Peace." His kingdom would always be at peace.

Lion: And so again I ask, what does that have to do with my dinner? Grrrrrr.

Sheep: Talk fast. He's beginning to drool.

Narrator: This person will rule his people with justice. Even the animals will live together in peace. Wolves and sheep, leopards and young goats. Calves and lion cubs. Cows and bears. Natural enemies will live in peace. They will all lie down together and children will be able to take care of them. Lions will even eat straw like the cows.

Lion: Oh yeah? Straw? Bleh! I prefer lamb chops.

Lamb: How do we know this person has come?

Donkey: I know. I carried his mother on my back, all the way to Bethlehem.

Innkeeper: When they got here, I didn't have room for them. But I found a space in my stable.

Cow: And I gave up my feed trough so that he would have a place to sleep.

Dove: And I kept watch all night.

Mary: (*Holding up a doll wrapped in cloth*) His name is Jesus. And he is my son.

Lamb: Baaa. Baaa. He's so little. But if he's going to be so important, why is he here in a stable? Kings are supposed to be born in palaces.

Joseph: He is a special baby. He is God's Son. God sent Jesus here to live like one of us.

Lion: But he's just a baby! Grrrrr!

Lamb: How can he bring peace to the whole world?

Mary: But he will grow up one day. And he will be a great teacher.

Joseph: And he will teach the people all about God.

Choose one or more activities to immerse your children in the Bible story.

Supplies:
blindfold

Zillies™:
none

What's in the Stable?

Bring the children together in a circle. Put one chair in the center.

Ask: What kinds of animals do you expect to find in a stable? (*Let the children list all the animals they think they might find.*) **Do you think it would be a good place to have a new baby?** (*no*)

Say: Let's play a game as we think about the place where baby Jesus was born. I will choose one of you to be IT. It will sit in the center of the circle blindfolded. I will choose people to come up and make the sound of some animal that might be found in a stable. Let's see if IT can guess who it is.

One at a time call children from the group. IT has three opportunities to guess who is making the sound. If IT guesses, then that person becomes the next IT. If IT can't guess, then choose another person to make an animal sound. This game is similar to a game played by boys and girls in Chile.

ZONE IN™

We can celebrate the birth of Jesus.

Hip Hop Hop

Create a hopscotch grid on the floor using masking tape. Instead of having double squares, have ten single squares in a line. The first square should be labeled "Nazareth". The last square should be labeled "Bethlehem." If you have a large class, have two grids and divide the children up.

Have each child in turn throw a single **foam die**. The child will then hop the number of squares shown on the dice. When the child lands on a square, he or she will do what the square indicates. The object is for each child to get from Nazareth to Bethlehem.

Say: We've all heard the story of the decree of Caesar Augustus where Joseph had to report to his home town to be counted. He took Mary with him. It was while they were in Bethlehem that it came time for Mary to have her baby. Jesus, the Son of God, was born in a stable because there was no room in the inn.

Supplies:
Reproducible 3B, scissors, masking tape

Zillies™:
foam dice.

Sing and Celebrate

Supplies:
cassette player

Zillies™:
Cassette

(M)ake a copy of the words for each child. Let the children use their hands or feet to make the sound of the donkey on the refrain.

That First Christmas Night

The stars were bright on that first Christmas night,
Mary and Joseph came traveling.
For many days and from far away
Mary and Joseph came traveling.

REFRAIN 1:
Clip, Clop, Clippity, clop;
Mary and Joseph were traveling.
Clip, Clop, Clippity, clop;
Mary and Joseph were traveling.

The stars were bright on that first Christmas night,
Mary and Joseph came into town.
They found out soon that there was no room,
Mary and Joseph came into town.

REFRAIN 1

The stars were bright on that first Christmas night,
Jesus was born in a cattle stall.
Bringing joy was this heav'nly boy,
Jesus was born in a cattle stall.

REFRAIN 2
Clip, Clop, Clippity, clop;
Jesus was born in a cattle stall.
Clip, Clop, Clippity, clop;
Jesus was born in a cattle stall.

REFRAIN 1 (Repeat)
Mary and Joseph were traveling.
(Repeat after last line)

Supplies:
masking tape,
open space

Zillies™:
none

St. Lucia's Scramble

Say: On December 13, the Christmas season officially begins in Sweden with St. Lucia's Day. Early that morning the eldest girl in the family dresses in a white gown with a red sash. On her head she wears a wreath of evergreens and candles. The girl goes from room to room, waking the family and delivering a special breakfast. According to legend, Lucia was a Christian girl who lived a long time ago. At this time the Romans hunted down and killed anyone they found that was Christian. So the Christians had to hide from the Romans. Lucia risked her life to bring food and water to the Christians. So that her hands were free to carry the food, she wore candles on her head.

Divide the children into two groups. Two children will be the Romans. The remaining children will be the Christians. With masking tape, draw a line and position all the Christians behind the line. The Romans are to keep watch so that the Christians do not escape. Select one of the Christians to be Lucia. Lucia will be out of the group. It is Lucia's job to run across the area and tag a fellow Christian. That Christian is then free and can help Lucia save the other Christians.

Say: When Jesus was born it was a very dangerous time. The Romans ruled the world. The Jewish people had been waiting and hoping for a Savior. And now he was here.

Supplies:
none

Zillies™:
inflatable bell

Ring Out the News

Have the children form a prayer circle. Hold the **bell** out in front and let each child place his or her hands on the **bell.** This might mean that you have a very tight circle if you have a large group.

When everyone is touching the **bell, pray:** Dear God, we thank you for your gift of Jesus. Help us to remember Jesus in everything we do as we prepare to celebrate his birthday. Amen.

Ask: **What's the good news?** (*Jesus is born!*) **What did you say?** (*Jesus is born!*) **I still can't hear you!** (*Jesus is born!*)

On the third response, toss the **bell** up into the air, and let everyone cheer.

Make a copy of HomeZone™ for each family in the class.

Bible Verse
Mary gave birth to her firstborn son and wrapped him in bands of cloth, and laid him in a manger.
Luke 2:7, adapted

Bible Story
Luke 2:1-7

In today's Bible story your child heard about the birth of Jesus. How often we glamorize the idea of being born in a stable and sleeping on soft clean hay. But I think we can assume that this was not the case. God sent Jesus to live among human beings, so that Jesus could experience life as one of us. What a gift to give. Take time to celebrate with your child. Include him or her in the events that make the holiday season special. Remind your child that Jesus came into the world as a little baby. He had parents who cared for him and provided for him. We can celebrate God's gift of Jesus.

Punched Tin Ornaments

Punched tin is a special craft often found in Mexico or Central America. Make special ornaments for your tree. Hang this on the door.

Supplies: aluminum pie plate, recycled newspapers, nail, hammer, pre-gathered Christmas trim, colored yarn, white paper, pencil, permanent markers, tape.

1. Trace around the bottom of each pie tin on a piece of white paper. Cut out. This becomes the template for the punched tin design.
2. Create a design using pencil dots. Make it as simple or as elaborate as you want.
3. Poke through each dot in the design with a sharp pencil. Tape the design to the inside of the pie plate. Then use permanent markers to transfer the hole pattern to the pie plate.
4. Place the pie pan on the stack of newspaper on the floor. Have an adult hold the pan while the child uses a hammer and nail to punch through each dot.
5. Punch two holes, side by side, at the top of the plate. Thread a length of yarn through the holes and tie to form a hanger.
6. Glue the pre-gathered Christmas trim under the edge of the pie plate.

Hang as a greeting for all Christmas visitors.

Zone In

We can celebrate Jesus' birth.

Reproducible 3A

BIBLEZONE™

Move up 1.

Move up 1.

Lose a turn.

Go back 2.

Go back 1.

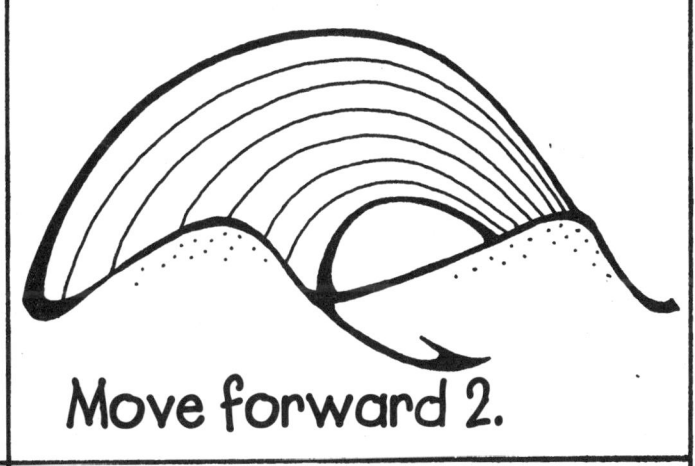

Move forward 2.

Move up 2.

Lose a turn.

Reproducible 3B

Shepherds Kept Watch

Enter the ZONE™

Bible Verse
To you is born this day in the city of David a Savior, who is the Messiah, the Lord.
Luke 2:11

Bible Story
Luke 2:8–20

The Scriptures tell us that the first to hear the good news of Jesus' birth were humble shepherds. God chose to proclaim the birth of God's son not to kings and emperors, but rather to people in the most lowly of positions. God's greatest gift is for all people regardless of their position in life. God's call comes to everyone.

The fields around Bethlehem do not grow lush with grass. In order for their sheep to graze, shepherds moved them about during the day. At night the shepherds drove the sheep to a common place for protection. Sometimes the sheep were kept in a sheepfold. This was either an enclosure built with a wall of rocks or a shelter built into a cave. One shepherd would lie down across the opening so that the sheep would not wander out during the night. Jesus often compared himself to a shepherd looking after sheep, and once as the door to the sheepfold.

Shepherds were simple, hardworking people. The religious leaders in the Jewish community looked down on the shepherds. Because of the very nature and difficulty of their work with the flocks, shepherds were not able to observe all the details of ceremonial law. For instance, it was impossible for them to follow all the rules and regulations of meticulous hand washing and food handling.

The shepherds were probably surprised that the Savior had been born into a peasant family and that his birth was announced first to people of lowly birth. The angel's song makes it clear -- God's peace is for all.

For children the time leading up to our celebration of the Savior's birth can be anything but peaceful. Continue to plan for some quiet activities for children who might be over-stressed. Children live in a world of wonder. As you prepare this lesson, think about the story from a child's perspective. What amazes you? Angel songs? The baby? You as the teacher can convey a message of awe and expectation—similar to that experienced by those shepherds in the field.

We celebrate the shepherds who were the first to hear about Jesus' birth.

Scope the ZONE ™

ZONE	TIME	SUPPLIES	⊚ ZILLIES™
Zoom Into the Zone			
Let's Be Shepherds	15 minutes	one-yard square of plain muslin for each child, yellow and white crayons, plastic dishpans, food coloring, iron, recycled newspapers, water, old towels	none
BibleZone™			
Wolf! Wolf!	5 minutes	none	none
The Night That Was Different	5 minutes	none	lamb puppet
Naciementos	15 minutes	Reproducibles 4A and 4B, shoeboxes, construction paper, crayons or felt-tip markers, glue, tape, dried straw or grass, natural items	none
LifeZone			
Sing About Christmas	5 minutes	cassette player	Cassette
Come to the Manger	5 minutes	shoebox, small doll, strips of cloth	gold shred
Hallelujah Signs	5 minutes	none	none

⊚ Zillies™ are found in the **BibleZone™ FUNspirational™** Kit.

Choose one or more activities to catch your children's interest.

one-yard square of plain muslin for each child, yellow and white crayons, plastic dishpans, food coloring, iron, recycled newspapers, water. old towels

Zillies™:
none

Let's Be Shepherds

Cut a one-yard square of plain muslin for each child. Cover the tables with newspaper. Set out yellow and white crayons. If you have a large class, instead of making the headdress, make head ties. Each child will need a six-inch by thirty-six inch strip of fabric instead. Place water in each of the three dishpans. Add food coloring until the water is an intense color. Set the dishpans on tables covered with newspaper.

Greet the children as they arrive. Give each child the square (or strip) of muslin.

Say: **Today we are going to be shepherds. Shepherds played an important role in the story of Jesus' birth. In order to be good shepherds, we have to look like shepherds. In order to look like shepherds, we need to have headdresses. We are going to decorate our headdresses using a technique called Batik.**

Let the children create a simple design with the yellow or white crayons. Then dip the fabric in one of the dishpans of water and food coloring. Use a spoon to swish the fabric around. Continue swishing until the fabric is the color you want. Remove the fabric from the color bath and dip into the clear water. Wring out and then place the fabric between sheets of newspaper or old towels and blot. If you have time, repeat this process with another color of dye. Iron the fabric dry. Change the newspaper frequently to absorb the wax. The design will show through the colors.

When the time comes to wear the headdress, make a tie to secure it in place. Old silk ties, braided yarn, and clean discarded panty hose make good ties. Tie around each child's head securing the headdress in place.

We celebrate the shepherds who were the first to hear of Jesus' birth.

Bible ZONE™

Choose one or more activities to immerse your children in the Bible story.

Wolf! Wolf!

Supplies:
Bible

Zillies™:
none

Say: Today's Bible story is about the shepherds who came heard the good news of Jesus' birth and came to find him. The Bible talks a great deal about shepherds. They were a common sight in Palestine at that time. It was their job to take care of the sheep of the village. One part of the job was to protect the sheep from hungry animals who wanted lamb for dinner. When Jesus grew up he compared God's love and care to that of the shepherd.

You may want to read some of the scriptures that refer to shepherds. (*Psalm 23, Psalm 100, John 10:11, Luke 2: 8, Hebrews 13:20*)

Say: Let's play a game where we can understand just how hard it was to be a shepherd in Bible times. One of you will be the wolf who is very hungry. One of you will be the shepherd whose job is to protect the sheep from the wolf. The rest of you will be sheep.

Select one child to be the shepherd and one child to be the wolf. The rest of the children will line up behind the shepherd. Each child will hold onto the shoulders of the child in front of him or her. The wolf wants the juicy lamb at the end of the line.

Say: When I say "go," the wolf is going to try to catch the lamb at the end of the line. If the wolf is able to grab onto the waist of the lamb, then the lamb is caught. It is up to all the other sheep and the shepherd to try to protect the lamb without letting go of one another. When the lamb is caught, the wolf takes it back to its den and the next to the last person becomes the one the wolf is after.

This game is similar to a game played in Turkey called Tilki ve Tavuk (Fox and Hen) and one played in China called Lao Yin Chuo Siao Chi (Eagle and Chickens.)

Bring the children back to the circle.

Say: Even though the shepherd played an important job in the village, the people did not think very much of them. They were the lowest of the low on the social scale. I wonder why God chose them to be the very first to hear the good news.

ZONE IN™ | **We celebrate the shepherds who were the first to hear of Jesus' birth.**

The Night That Was Different

by Sharilyn S. Adair

Today's story is done as a monologue by one of the shepherds who was out on that hillside in Bethlehem. The shepherd relates the story to villagers around the campfire. Invite an adult from the church to play the part of the shepherd. Provide appropriate shepherd's clothing. Accompanying the shepherd is a lamb. Select one of the children to be the first lamb. After each response, the child will pass the lamb to the person on the right. The response is "Baaa!" But each time the lamb responds it should be with the emotion the child thinks is appropriate to the story that is being told.

Let the children wear the headdresses they made. Create a campfire from a box lid, wooden sticks, white Christmas lights, and colored tissue paper (red, orange, yellow.) Have the children gather around the campfire. Create an atmosphere of mystery and awe.

Shepherd: Let me tell you about a night that was like no other night before it or any night since.

Lamb: Baaa!

Shepherd: It was very late. The sheep were all settled for the night. There was not a single creature stirring.

Lamb: Baaa!

Shepherd: I was so tired that night. I had just laid down across the sheepfold gate to keep the sheep in for the night. I stretched out and looked up at the stars.

Lamb: Baaa!

Shepherd: See, the same stars that were there that night are here tonight. But now, everything is different. Look! See the Great Bear.

Lamb: Baaa!

Shepherd: Instead of getting darker as I expected, the sky began to get lighter. That wasn't right. Soon the sky was so light that it was as though it were daylight.

Lamb: Baaa!

Shepherd: I called out to my friends. "Wake up! Wake up! Something is happening!"

Lamb: Baaa!

Shepherd: The light was so bright that I could barely look at it. (*Put arms over face as though shielding it from the bright light.*)

Lamb: Baaa!

Shepherd: We were all frightened. We did not understand what was happening. This had never happened to anyone else before. But then we heard a voice. "Do not be afraid."

Lamb: Baaa!

Shepherd: Not afraid? How could we not be afraid? Then I saw it. An angel. And the angel was talking to us. "I bring you good news of great joy for all the people. Today a Savior has been born, a Messiah, in the city of David."

Lamb: Baaa!

Shepherd: The Messiah! The Messiah has come. We have been waiting for years to hear this. And an angel brought us the good news.

Lamb: Baaa!

Shepherd: How will we know where to find this child? I asked the angel. And the angel said, "You will find the baby wrapped in bands of cloth and lying in a manger."

Lamb: Baaa!

Shepherd: Our Messiah, in a manger? Surely they were mistaken. A Messiah should come to a palace!

Lamb: Baaa!

Shepherd: Suddenly there was not just one angel but many. The sky was filled with their song, "Glory to God in the highest and peace to all people on earth."

Lamb: Baaa!

Shepherd: As quickly as the angels had appeared, they were gone. My friends and I decided we had to see what the angels were talking about.

Lamb: Baaa!

Shepherd: Something this important we had to see for ourselves. So we set off for Bethlehem to find this baby.

Lamb: Baaa!

Shepherd: When we got to Bethlehem, we searched until we found the stable. When we found it, there were Mary, Joseph, and the baby lying in the manger.

Lamb: Baaa!

Shepherd: We knelt beside the manger. This was the promised Messiah. This was the Savior God told us was coming. We knew because the angels told us.

Lamb: Baaa!

Shepherd: We told Mary all about the angels. As we left the city and went back to the hills, we told everyone we saw about the angels, the message, and the tiny baby sleeping in the manger.

Lamb: Baaa!

Bible Zone™

Choose one or more activities to immerse your children in the Bible story.

Supplies:
Reproducible 4A and 4B, shoe-boxes, construction paper, crayons or felt-tip markers, glue, tape, dried straw or grass, natural items

Zillies™:
none

Naciementos

Make a copy of the stable background *(Reproducible 4A)* and nativity figures *(Reproducible 4B)* for each child in the group. If you have a large class, let the children work in teams of two. Leave the nativity dioramas on display through Epiphany.

Ask: How many of you have a nativity set at home? When do you put it out? What figures does it have in it? Does it have a special place? When do you add baby Jesus/ When do you add the wise men?

Say: The very first nativity display was done in 1223 or 1224 in Italy by a village priest named Francis. He discovered that most of the people of his village were poor and could neither read nor write. So, they did not know the Christmas story. Francis decided to recreate the story in a cave behind the village. He used real people to play the parts of Mary, Joseph and the shepherds. Now people all over the world have nativity scenes. Each is different and shows the event as they picture it. In Mexico the nativity scene is called a *naciemento*. Let's each of us make a *naciemento*.

Have the children color the stable background and glue it into the bottom of a shoebox turned on its side. Then add the figures and any other items to make the scene more realistic.

We celebrate the shepherds who were the first to hear the good news.

52

BIBLEZONE™

Life Tone™

Choose one or more activities to bring the Bible to life.

Supplies:
cassette player

Zillies™:
Cassette

Sing About Christmas

Make a copy of the words for each child. This song has a Dixieland feel to it. Have the children wave their hands overhead during the refrain. When they come to the phrase "glory hallelujah" let them stand up.

Hallelujah Song

Hallelujah, you could hear the people sing
when they heard the news about the new-born King.
What a joyful night it was in Bethlehem
when the Son of God came down to men!
"Hallelujah, halelu," the angels sang,
till the very highest courts of heaven rang.
Cherubim and seraphim in one accord
were gathered there to praise the Lord.
They sang. . .

REFRAIN:
Hal-le, hal-le-lu-jah, (glory hal-le-lu-jah!)
Ha-le-, ha-le-lu, ha-le-lu-jah
glory ha-le-lu-jah.
Hal-le, hal-le-lu-jah, (glory hal-le-lu-jah!)
Hal-le, ha-le-lu (glory ha-le-lu!)
Ha-le-lu, ha-le-lu-(Ha-le--lu-jah!) (Second Repeat Only)

Shepherds came from miles around to see the sight.
Wise men followed right behind the star so bright.
When they heard the music of the angel band,
they sang along and clapped their hands.
All around the manger where the baby lay,
even lowly creatures seemed to swing and sway.
If they could, I know they would have joined the throng,
singing that hallelujah song.
They sang . . .

REFRAIN (2nd Repeat)

Now, ev'erybody sing that hal-le-lu-jah,
ev'erybody sing that hal-le-lu-jah,
ev'erybody sing that hal-le-lu-jah song!

Life Zone™

Choose one or more activities to bring the Bible to life.

Come to the Manger

(F)ill the shoebox with the gold shred. Wrap the baby doll in bands of cloth and place the doll in the shoebox.

Ask: Who can come to the manger to worship baby Jesus?

Choose a characteristic that several children possess. Invite them to come to the manger. Let the rest of the children try to identify the criteria. Then have that group leave. Invite another group of children. Repeat the procedure. Do this until everyone has had the chance to come to the manger at least one time.

Say: The good news of Jesus' birth came first to lowly shepherds in the fields. They stopped what they were doing to find the baby. God invites all of us to come to the manger and worship the baby Jesus.

Hallelujah Signs

(T)each the children the American Sign Language below.

Say: When the shepherds left the stable, they told everyone they met about the tiny baby and the angels. We can tell others about Jesus, too.

Pray: Thank you, God for the shepherds who were the first to hear about baby Jesus. (*Sign the phrase.*) **Thank you, God for Christmas when we celebrate Jesus' birthday.** (*Sign the phrase.*) **Thank you for the people all over the world who celebrate Jesus' birthday.** (*Sign the phrase.*) **Amen.**

Make a copy of HomeZone™ for each family in your class.

Home Zone For Parents

Bible Verse
To you is born this day in the city of David a Savior, who is the Messiah, the Lord.
Luke 2:11

Bible Story
Luke 2:8–20

In today's Bible story your child heard the story of the shepherds and the angels. God's Son was announced not to the royalty of Palestine, but to the lowly shepherds who were keeping watch on their sheep on a cold and windy hillside. Help your child understand that God sent Jesus into the world for all people, not just those people who are like us. The whole world celebrates Jesus' birthday, each country in its own special ways. The whole world welcomes Jesus.

The Candy Cane

Take a good look at the candy cane. What does it remind you of? Of course, it looks like a shepherd's crook. Many, many years ago a candy maker wanted to celebrate the birth of Jesus in a very special way. So he designed a candy that would celebrate the shepherd's visit to the stable.

Make Candy Cane Cookies

Ingredients: ½ cup shortening, ½ cup margarine, 1 cup confectioners sugar, 1 egg, 1 ½ teaspoons almond extract, 1 teaspoon vanilla, 2 ½ cups flour, 1 teaspoon salt

Cream together shortening, margarine, and confectioners sugar. Add egg, almond extract and vanilla. Sift together flour and salt. Gradually add this to the creamed mixture. Divide the dough in half. Add ½ teaspoon of red food coloring to half the dough. Squeeze color into dough with hands. Roll a tablespoon of each color dough into 2- to 3-inch strips. Place a red and a white strip side by side on a cookie sheet. Twist together, like a rope, curving the top to form a cane. Bake in a preheat oven at 350 degrees for about nine minutes. Remove before the cookies get brown. While hot, sprinkle with a mixture of ½ cup granulated sugar and ½ cup confectioners sugar sifted together. Makes about four dozen cookies.

We celebrate the shepherd's who were the first to hear of Jesus' birth.

Reproducible 4A

BibleZone™

Reproducible 4A

Simeon and Anna

Enter the ZONE™

Bible Verse
. . . Lord, you have kept your promise. . .
Luke 2:29, *Good News Bible*

Bible Story
Luke 2:25–39

Luke seems to have combined two Old Testament rituals, the ceremony of purification and the redemption of the first-born. Forty days following the birth of her child, a woman was required to offer a sacrifice consisting of a lamb, or for a poor woman, a pair of turtledoves, or two young pigeons. This was the ceremony of purification. According to Jewish custom, the first-born boy in a family belonged to the Lord and must be redeemed with an offering of five shekels. This offering was made by the father in a ceremony called the redemption of the firstborn. It is certainly possible, of course, that Mary and Joseph themselves combined the two rituals. The important thing is that they were together at the temple – or more likely in the temple courtyard, since both Mary and Anna were present. (Women were not allowed within the Temple proper.)

In Luke's account, Simeon, an aged prophet, has been awaiting the birth of the Messiah. Amidst the hundreds of paid priests, sacrificers, musicians, treasurers, and the like, Simeon sees Mary and Joseph and the baby. It is clear to him that his hopes have been fulfilled. Taking the baby in his arms, he sings a song of praise and thanksgiving and then offers a special blessing to Mary.

At the same time we are introduced to Anna, a prophetess who had lived in the temple, fasting and praying day and night for most of her adult life. She too begins to praise God for the birth of a baby who will lead his people to salvation.

For children special celebrations always seem to have attached to them a time of waiting. They wait for Christmas, wait for their birthdays, and wait for visits from special relatives. Imagine being a person during Bible times who was waiting for the Messiah. The people who were waiting for the Messiah had been waiting not for days or months, but for years. And yet their hope never wavered. God had promised and God always keeps promises.

Jesus is the promised Savior.

Scope the ZONE ™

ZONE	TIME	SUPPLIES	☉ ZILLIES™
Zoom Into the Zone			
After-Christmas Cards	15 minutes	Reproducible 5B, crayons or felt-tip markers, glue or tape, ½ inch cardboard squares	none
I Don't Think So!	10 minutes	six brown paper lunch bags	pom-poms, friction car, glitter balls, lion puppet, gold shred, foam dice
BibleZone™			
Take It Off!	10 minutes	Reproducible 5A, construction paper, scissors, tape, felt-tip marker	foam dice
I Have Seen the Lord!	5 minutes	none	none
Who Is It?	10 minutes	none	jewel light
LifeZone			
Sing and Celebrate	5 minutes	cassette player	Cassette
Promise Signs	5 minutes	Bibles, index cards, permanent felt-tip markers	none

☉ Zillies™ are found in the **BibleZone™ FUNspirational™ Kit.**

Zoom Into the

Choose one or more activities to catch your children's interest.

Supplies:
Reproducible 5B, crayons or felt-tip markers, glue or tape, ½ inch cardboard squares

Zillies™:
none

After-Christmas Cards

Make a copy of the after-Christmas card for each child in the group. If you have extended time, children may make more than one.

Greet the children as they arrive. Direct them to a table where you have set out the materials for the after-Christmas Cards *(Reproducible 5B)*.

Let the children begin work on the cards. Show the children how to attach small cardboard squares to the backs of the figures to create three-dimensional figures for the after-Christmas cards.

Say: It may seem unusual to be sending Christmas cards after Christmas. But Christmas is only the beginning. From the day of Jesus' birth, special things began to happen.

Jesus is the promised Savior.

Supplies:
six brown paper lunch bags

Zillies™:
pom poms, friction car, glitter balls, lion puppet, gold shred, foam dice

I Don't Think So!

Prior to class, number or letter each of the brown paper lunch bags. Put one of these items in each bag: pom poms, friction car, glitter balls, lion puppet, gold shred.

Bring the children together in a circle.

Say: Here are six bags. I have something in each bag. I am going to hold up each bag and name an object. I will call on one of you. You can come and inspect the bag in any way except open it. Then you will respond with either "Absolutely" or "I don't think so."

Ask: Could you tell what was in each bag by just looking at it? Could you tell what was in each bag by lifting it? Could you tell what was in each bag by shaking it?

Say: In today's Bible story two people identify the promised Messiah just by looking at him. I wonder how they knew?

Bible Zone™

Choose one or more activities to immerse your children in the Bible story.

Take It Off!

Make a copy of the picture of Mary, Joseph and the baby Jesus (*Reproducible 5A*). Trim a piece of construction paper so that it completely covers the picture. Then cut the construction paper into puzzle pieces of various sizes. Make sure there are no more than twelve pieces. Number each piece randomly. Put a loop of tape on the back of each piece and reassemble on top of the illustration. Place the illustration on the wall or on a table where all the children can see it.

Say: Here is a special picture. Everyone of you will recognize it when you see it.

Ask: What do you think it is? (*You can't tell.*) Why can't you tell? (*It's covered up.*) How will we discover what's there? (*Remove the pieces.*)

Divide the children into two teams— Team A and Team B.

Say: I will ask a question of Team A. The team can confer on the answer. But the spokesperson can give only one answer for the team. If Team A answers correctly, then the team rolls the dice and removes the piece of the puzzle with that number on it. (*Later in the game if that number has already been removed, then the turn passes to the next team.*) Team A then has ten seconds to decide what picture is under the puzzle pieces. If Team A cannot guess in that length of time, I will ask a question of Team B. To remove a puzzle piece, the team must answer a question correctly. If the answer to the question is incorrect, then Team B gets the opportunity to answer. The first team that decides who or what is in the picture wins the game. (*Note: If your children enjoy this game, you can play it with other drawings and illustrations as well.*)

After the game is finished, ask the children: What gave the picture away? How many puzzle pieces were left when the game was won? How did you know what the picture was?

Say: In today's Bible story two people have been waiting a long time for someone to show up. When that person did appear, those who were waiting knew the special one right away!

Zone In™: Jesus is the promised savior.

Supplies:
Reproducible 5A, construction paper, scissors, tape, felt-tip marker

Zillies™:
foam dice

I Have Seen the Lord!

by Sharilyn S. Adair

> **T**oday's story-poem can be told with a background of rhythmic clapping. Teach students these hand movements to a steady beat of ten counts with a pause at the end of every two lines of poetry. On the words snap, snap, students are to snap their fingers first with one hand and then with the other:
>
> Clap, snap, snap, clap, snap, snap
> clap, clap, clap, clap (pause)
> Clap, snap, snap, clap, snap, snap
> clap, clap, clap, clap (pause)
>
> When students are clapping and snapping in rhythm, begin reading the story-poem.

Simeon, Simeon
faithful and true
God has a blessing
especially for you.

Though you are old and your
life journey's done,
you shall not die till you've
seen God's own Son.

Now in the Temple you
look for a sign
Led by God's Spirit to
seek the divine.

Parents and baby are
coming your way.
You take the child; then you
praise God and say:

"Lord, let your servant in
peace now depart.
These eyes have seen what I
know in my heart.

"Here is salvation, your
name now be praised."
Joseph and Mary are
watching, amazed.

Anna, the prophet, you
also have come.
You too can see what is
hidden from some.

Many long years you have
fasted and prayed?
What you've been seeking's no
longer delayed.

"See the Messiah!" you
counsel the crowd,
voicing thanksgiving and
praises aloud.

Anna and Simeon,
you've both been blessed.
Now, as the family de-
parts, you can rest.

The people have waited
for years it is true.
God's promise to send a
Messiah came true.

Choose one or more activities to immerse your children in the Bible story.

Supplies:
none

Zillies™:
jewel light

Who Is It?

Bring the children together in an open area. Select one child to be IT and the rest of the children will form a line behind her or him.

Say: Simeon and Anna both believed God's promise that a Messiah was coming. They didn't know what the Messiah would look like. All they knew was that they would know this person on sight. Who would have thought that it would be a little tiny baby. Let's play a game and see if we can recognize someone just by a verbal description.

This game is very similar to a game played by the children in Chile called "Who Is It?" The game begins as the child who is IT passes the jewel light over his or her shoulder. The children in the line continue passing it back and forth until IT says "Stop." Whoever has the light comes and stands directly behind IT who is facing away from the group. The group chants: Who is it? Who is it? Who is it?

IT responds by asking three questions, all of which can be answered by a Yes or a No. For example, IT may ask: Is it a boy? Is the person tall? Is the person wearing a green shirt? Then IT must guess who is standing behind her or him. If IT guesses correctly, then IT has another turn. If IT guesses incorrectly, another child becomes IT.

Jesus is the promised Savior.

Sing and Celebrate

Supplies:
cassette player

Zillies™:
Cassette

Make a copy of the words for the children or create a song chart for use in the front of the class. This song has a Caribbean sound. Remind the children that people around the world celebrate Christmas in their own ways. Children may want to form a conga line (one right behind the other, connected by hands on the waist. Move around the room in a line as you sing).

The Virgin Mary Had a Baby Boy

De Virgin Mary had a baby boy:
De Virgin Mary had a baby boy:
De Virgin Mary had a baby boy:
They said that His name was Jesus.

De angels sang when de baby was born.
De angels sang when de baby was born.
De angels sang when de baby was born.
They said that His name was Jesus.

REFRAIN:
He come from de glory,
He come from de glorious kingdom.
He come from de glory.
He come from de glorious kingdom.

REFRAIN (Repeat)

Supplies:
  Bibles, eight index
    cards, perma-
    nent felt-tip
    marker

Zillies™:
  none

Promise Signs

On the index cards write the following Scripture references: John 3:16, 1 John 1:9, Genesis 28:15, Genesis 9:14–15, Isaiah 9:6, Luke 1:30–31, Matthew 1:20–21, Luke 2:25–26. Give a card and a Bible to eight children. If your class is primarily beginning readers, use the index cards to mark the Scriptures and let children read an adapted version on each card. (For example, Luke 1:30–31—Mary will have a son. She will name him Jesus.)

Say: **Throughout the Bible God has made many promises to the people. We are part of those people today. I have marked some of the promises from the Bible. Let's listen to the promise and then if God kept the promise, let's sign the Bible verse.**

Teach the children the signs for the verse. Go over each carefully.

Lord, you keep your promise

Then take turns letting the children with Bibles and references read their Scriptures. After each Scripture, ask the children: Did God keep the promise? (The answer is yes to all the promises.)

Have the children form a prayer circle.

Pray: **Dear God, we thank you for your gift of Jesus. You always keep your promises to us. Amen.**

Make a copy of HomeZone™ for each family in your class.

Bible Verse
. . . Lord, you have kept your promise. . .
Luke 2:29, *Good News Bible*

Bible Story
Luke 2:25–39

In today's story your child heard about Simeon and Anna, among the first people to recognize Jesus as the promised Messiah. Both waited at the Temple. Simeon had been promised that he would see the promised one before he died. And Anna recognized the baby on sight. This brings up an interesting question. How did they know? And would we know if we had been the ones waiting for God's special gift? How many special people do we not see because we are not anxiously awaiting the special and the divine?

LifeZone
Just because Christmas Day is over does not mean that Christmas should not go on all year round. Help your child to discover "gifts" he or she can give—gifts of service to friends and family members.

Recycled Trees
Don't just throw out your live Christmas tree when the needles begin to drop—recycle it! Make it a Christmas tree for the birds. This time make all the ornaments edible.

Popcorn and Cranberry chains: Birds love snacks during the cold dark days of winter. With a yarn needle and heavy quilting thread, string popcorn kernels and cranberries and drape them over the branches.

Pinecone Pizazz: Spread peanut butter in and around the layers of the pine cone. Tie with yarn and hang from the branches.

Feather The Nest: Leave bits of colored yarn and tinsel for the birds to use in their nesting material.

Bread Cookies: Use Christmas cookie cutters to cut shapes from stale bread. Hang them from the tree.

Orange Cups: Fill scooped out orange halves with suet and seed.

Jesus is the promised Savior.

68

Reproducible 5A

Merry Christmas all year long

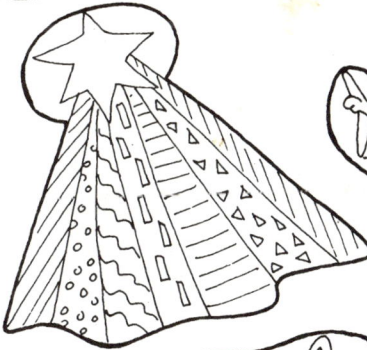

Reproducible 5B

69

Follow that Star!

Enter the Zone™

Bible Verse

When they saw that the star had stopped, they were overwhelmed with joy.
Matthew 2:10

Bible Story
Matthew 2:1–12

The Hebrew people lived in a time of great darkness. They were oppressed by the many conqueror nations who used their tiny nation as a land bridge. But they never lost the hope that God would send a Savior, one to free the oppressed, heal the sick, and bring comfort to the poor. Because of this sense of darkness, readers often find the image of Jesus as light in the Bible.

In the Nativity stories we find another image of light. However, this time the light comes not to the Hebrew people, but to all people everywhere. In the story of the wise men, we find scholars from foreign lands who see the star and immediately follow the star's light as they seek the new king. Again, out of the darkness comes a light that provides guidance. The significance of this story falls not in the fact that people from far away came to find the new Savior, but that these men were Gentiles. God was made known to all people through Jesus. The church celebrates this revelation with Epiphany, which begins on January 6 and lasts until Ash Wednesday.

In this time after Christmas be prepared for children to boast about their Christmas gifts. Rather than avoid talk of gifts, use this oppor- tunity to talk about appreciation for gifts. Gift- giving is a response to the news of Jesus and a celebration of his birth. It is a chance to reflect the love God has shown us.

Children also may be experiencing after- Christmas blues as a feeling of letdown that Christmas is over. Encourage children to remember and to tell the story of Christmas throughout the year.

The fact that Gentiles claimed and wor- shiped the Savior had to be made acceptable to the Jewish people. Likewise, acceptance is an important issue for first- and second- graders. Peer acceptance is becoming a major factor in their enjoyment of school or other social events. Being "in" or "out" is sometimes only a matter of a particular item of clothing or a special toy.

Help children understand that they are all God's children—loved and accepted as they are. Jesus was God's gift to the world—not to just one certain group of people. Today's lesson is a good time to talk about outreach to people who are perceived as different. Help the children to focus on the similarities among people, rather than the differences.

God was made known to all people through Jesus.

Scope the ZONE™

ZONE	TIME	SUPPLIES	☉ ZILLIES™
Zoom Into the Zone			
Let There Be Light	15 minutes	Reproducible 6A, scissors, black construction paper, toothpicks or sharpened pencils, paper punches, glass jars, tea candles or small votive candles	none
Star Scramble	5 minutes	Reproducibles 6A and 6B, scissors, masking tape, cassette player, resealable plastic bags	Cassette, pom-poms
BibleZone™			
Give Me a Sign	10 minutes	three sheets of paper, felt-tip marker, pointer or yardstick.	lion puppet, lamb puppet, friction car
Too Many Kings!	10 minutes	clothing for King Herod, chair covering, crown if available	kazoos
Color Chaos	10 minutes	masking tape	pom-poms
LifeZone			
Sing and Celebrate	5 minutes	cassette player, musical instruments if available	Cassette, metallic streamers
Gifts of Love	5 minutes	none	prism gift bag, metallic gold shred

☉ Zillies™ are found in the **BibleZone™ FUNspirational™ Kit.**

Zoom Into the ZONE™

Choose one or more activities to catch your children's interest.

Supplies:

Reproducible 6A,
scissors, black
construction
paper, tooth-
picks or sharp-
ened pencils,
paper punches,
glass jars, tea
candles or small
votive candles

Zillies™:

Let There Be Light

Make a copy of the luminaria pattern *(Reproducible 6A)* for each child. Cut off the words on the right. Save to use in the next activity. Cut strips of black construction paper just slightly wider than the pattern for each child.

Greet the children as they arrive. Direct them to a work table. Show them how to tape the pattern on the construction paper. Demonstrate how to use a toothpick or a sharpened pencil to poke a hole at each point indicated on the pattern. Then remove the pattern and re-punch the holes using a paper punch.

Say: The Bible often uses the word light to mean Jesus. For many years, the people suffered under Roman rule. God promised to send the people a Savior; Jesus was that Savior. Jesus gave the people hope. Jesus brought light into a dark world. In today's story the light comes not just to the Hebrew people, but to all people.

Tape the ends of the luminaria to form a tube. Slip it over a small glass jar. Place a tea candle or a small votive candle in the jar and light it. Watch the light shine through.

Supplies:

Reproducibles 6A
and 6B, scissors,
masking tape,
cassette player,
resealable plas-
tic bags

Zillies™:

Cassette, pom-
poms

Star Scramble

Make enough copies of the star pattern *(Reproducible 6B)* for each child in your class. Cut apart the words *(Reproducible 6A)* and tape or glue one word to each star. Each word stands for an astronomical event or object. Scatter the stars randomly around the room. Make an extra copy of the words. Cut them apart and put them in a basket.

Give each child a resealable bag with five pom-poms. (Size is irrelevant.)

Say: Long ago people watched the sky for unusual events or objects. These events or objects were thought to mean different things. A new star, for example, meant that a king was born. Scattered around the room are stars. The words on the stars are things you might see if you were an astronomer. As I play music (Cassette) I want you to move around the room. When the music stops, I will draw a word from the basket. Anyone who is standing on a star with that word receives a pom-pom. All others have to pay a pom-pom to the basket. When you are out of pom-poms, you are out of the game. The person at the end of the game with the most pom-poms wins.

Bible ZONE™

Choose one or more activities to immerse your children in the Bible story.

Give Me a Sign

Before class begins today, select one of the children to be in on the trick to this game. If you have a very young group of children, you may want to ask another adult to participate instead.

Write one of these letters on one of three plain sheets of paper: C, A, R. Place the sheets of paper on the floor. Have the children form a circle with the three pieces of paper in the center. Place the lion puppet on C, the lamb puppet on A, and the car on R.

Say: In today's Bible story we are going to hear about a secret sign, a sign that told some people who study the stars that a new king had been born. I wonder how they knew. Let's play a game where there is a secret sign. Only (name of child) and I know what it is. See if you can discover what it is.

Secret sign: The words the leader uses to call the child back to the group will identify which item has been chosen. "Come back" means the group has chosen the item on C. "All right" means the group has chosen the item on A. "Ready!" means the group has chosen the item on R.

Say: Pay close attention.

Have the selected child leave the circle or turn away. Have one of the children select one of the items. Then recall the child to the group using the secret code. (*Come in, All right, Ready*)

Ask: Which item do you think the group has chosen?

Do this several times so that the children are totally mystified and trying to discover the secret code. If no one figures it out, let the child explain it to the group.

Say: IT was listening for a special sign to help him/her know which item the group had chosen. In today's Bible story some scholars were watching for a secret sign as well. When they saw the new star, they knew that a new king had been born. This king was not just for one group of people or country; this king had come for all people.

Supplies:
three sheets of paper, felt-tip marker, yardstick or pointer

Zillies™:
lion and lamb puppets, friction car

ZONE IN™

God was made known to all people through Jesus.

Too Many Kings!

by Sharilyn S. Adair and LeeDell Stickler

Invite a male adult from your church to relate the story of King Herod and the wise men. Provide a Roman-type toga and purple drape. A golden crown would also be appropriate. Drape a blanket over a chair to serve as the throne. Encourage the storyteller to be dramatic. The children will become the "Greek Chorus." After each of Herod's speeches, the children will stand and repeat the lines indicated in the box below. Have them herald their speeches by using the kazoos to make trumpet sounds.

Say: We always tell the story of the wise men and their exciting journey to find the newborn king. But I wonder what it would have been like to be King Herod and know that something wonderful was happening in Bethlehem.

**A star leads the way with its bright shining light
But there's too many kings in Palestine this night.**

Herod: (*Yawning*) It's much too early for a king to be awakened. How rude! And for such a trivial little problem. Some strangers are in town asking questions about another king. A new king. How ridiculous! I am the only king. How dare anyone even mention a new king!

Greek Chorus:

Herod: You see, if you don't stop these things before they get out of hand, they become impossible. These strangers have been getting everyone all stirred up. They keep asking everyone they see about a new king. It seems that they saw this new star one night. A new star means a new king has been born. People are always looking for signs of things to come. I'm so impressed.

Greek Chorus:

Herod: It just keeps getting worse. The latest news is that this star led these men to Jerusalem. Can you imagine tramping through the desert following a star? Give me a break! But I'll have to admit, I've never heard of a star acting like a road sign before. That's a new one. But I'm sure there's some explanation.

Greek Chorus:

Herod: I think I will check with my advisors. Surely somewhere in the Holy Scriptures I can find something that will convince these strange-looking fellows that there is no new king. They need to get a life.

Greek Chorus:

Herod: Well, my advisors weren't at all helpful. They are running around like crazy people. It seems that somewhere in some ancient scroll there is a prophecy about a Messiah coming. They really believe that the star may be a sign. And get this. Where do you think this new king is going to be born? Bethlehem, no less! Bethlehem is such a dinky little town! No self-respecting king would be born there.

Greek Chorus:

Herod: There appears to be more to all this than I thought at first. If all this is true, then I must find this new-born impostor and get rid of him. But how? I need a plan. I think I'll invite the travelers to the palace. I'll pretend to be interested in what they are doing. I'll tell them what I know and then have them go on their way. If that star is worth its salt, then I'm sure they'll find what they are looking for.

Greek Chorus:

Herod: Well, I sent those men on their way. They think they are going to Bethlehem as my ambassadors. When they find the new king they are going to send word back to me. Then instead of gold, I will send soldiers. They'll take care of this new king. Huh! No one can outsmart Herod the Great, the ruler of all of Palestine.

(At this point, take off the crown and speak in your normal voice.)

Herod was smart, but he was no match for God. After the wise men found Jesus and gave him their gifts, God warned them in a dream not to return to Herod. And so, rather than reporting back to King Herod, they went home by another route. King Herod never saw them again.

Note: To use the kazoos again, in the interest of health, take them home and soak them in soapy water. Rinse well and drain dry.

Choose one or more activities to immerse your children in the Bible story.

Supplies:
masking tape

Zillies™:
pom-poms

Color Chaos

Using masking tape create a space large enough for all the children to stand inside and have enough room to move about without bumping into each other. Divide the space in half. Scatter the pom-poms inside the space. Make sure there is a fairly even distribution of pom-poms.

Say: In Bible times people were either Jewish or non-Jewish. The non-Jewish people were called Gentiles. The Jewish people tried to have nothing to do with the Gentiles. They didn't talk with them. They didn't eat with them. They tried not to purchase anything from them at all. The Jewish people were expecting a Messiah. But because of this division, they thought that the Messiah would be coming just for them. And God did send Jesus to them, but God also sent Jesus to everybody else too.

Divide the children into Team A and Team B. Have Team A stand on one side of the room and Team B stand on the other side of the room. No team member can cross the dividing line. If a pompom goes out of bounds, the teacher places it back inside the line, near the area of the last person who touched it.

Say: I have some treats here. But I will only give them to the team that deserves them. The team that deserves them will be the team that has no yellow pompoms on their side of the room.

Give the children an opportunity to try to rid their side of yellow pompoms, knowing that both teams will be doing the same thing.

Say: Oh, no, I've changed my mind. The most deserving team will be the one that has no red pom-poms on its side of the room.

Do this several times with different colors. Then stop the game and have the children collect all the pom-poms and come to the circle. Pass out the treats to everyone.

Ask: Was it fair to judge a team based on what color pom-poms was on that team's side of the room? (*no*) **In this same way, do you think God sent Jesus to only one group of people?** (*no*)

> **God was made known to all people through Jesus.**

Life Zone ™

Choose one or more activities to bring the Bible to life.

Sing and Celebrate

Make a copy of the words for each of the children or create a song-chart for the group. If you have musical rhythm instruments, let the children use those as well. Explain to the children that in many countries they celebrate a time called Epiphany. This is the time when the wise men came to find the baby Jesus. Have a Three Kings Parade during worship. Use the metallic streamers as well as the instruments.

Supplies:
cassette player, musical instruments (if available)

Zillies™;
Cassette, metallic streamers

With a Star that Bright
Hoofbeats crossing the desert sand,
sounds of a mighty eastern caravan,
Hear the beat of the tambourines
on our way to see the newborn King.
With a star that bright, with a guiding light,
a very special King is born tonight.

Hear the drum and the tambourine,
Rat-tat-a-tat-a-tat-a,
Ching ching ching.
Lift your voices, join to sing,
"Al-le-lu-ia" to the newborn King.
La la la la la, la la la la la,
A very special King is born tonight.

Trumpets herald His majesty,
He'll be dressed in royal finery.
We'll see His palace fit for a King,
from our treasury His gifts we'll bring.
With a star that bright, with a guiding light,
a very special King is born tonight.
A very special King is born tonight.

Words by Karen Dean and Don Marsh
© 1984 New Spring Publishing, Inc. (ASCAP), a division of Brentwood-Benson Music Publishing, Inc.
All rights reserved. Used by Permission.
From *Kids Sing Christmas.*

Supplies:
none

Zillies™:
prism bag, metallic gold shred

Gifts of Love

Bring the children together in a circle. Give each child a small amount of the metallic gold shred.

Ask: What gifts did the wise men bring to baby Jesus? (*gold, frankincense, myrrh*)

Say: We cannot give Jesus such royal gifts, but each of us can give a gift of love in the coming week. God sent Jesus into the world to teach us about God and what God wants us to do. Jesus taught us that God wants us to love one another. I will pass the empty bag around the circle. As it comes to you, place your golden shred in the bag and tell something that you can do this week as a gift of love for someone else.

Pass the gift bag around the circle. Each person will pass it and ask the person next to him or her: What gift of love will you give Jesus this week?

When the bag has gone all the way around the circle, hold the bag up and then place it in the worship center.

Pray: Dear God, we thank you for your gift of Jesus. We have no gold, frankincense, or myrrh to give, but we can give a gift of love to others. Amen.

ZONE IN™

God was made known to all people through Jesus.

Make a copy of HomeZone for each family in your class.

Bible Verse
When they saw that the star had stopped, they were overwhelmed with joy.
Matthew 2:10

Bible Story
Matthew 2:1–12

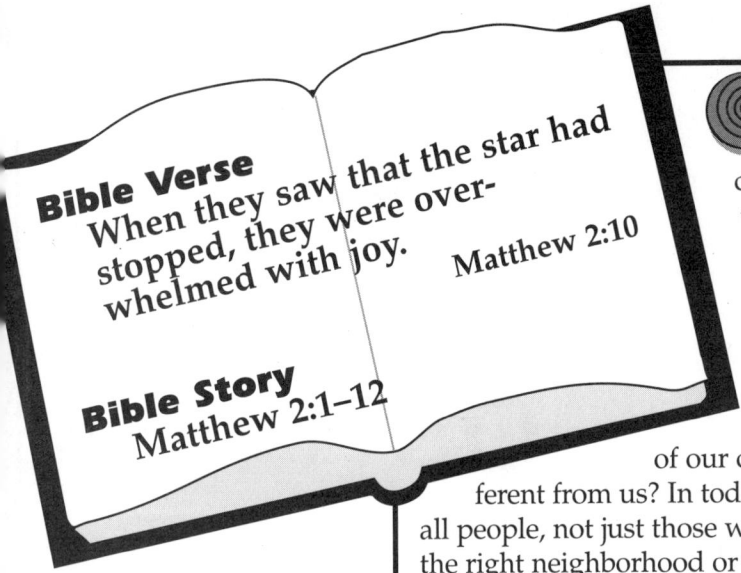

In today's Bible story your child heard about the visit of the wise men to the child Jesus. This story had great significance to the people who heard it because it indicated a big change. The wise men were Gentiles. Jesus was not just the Messiah to the Jewish people; he was the Messiah and Savior of all people. This was not easy for the people to accept. The Gentiles were social outcasts. How often do we close the doors of our church in subtle ways to people who are different from us? In today's story your child heard that Jesus came to all people, not just those with the right kind of clothing or who live in the right neighborhood or who are acceptable in our lives.

Visit a Planetarium
Today we know so much more about the heavens than did the people of Bible times. But still the stars remain something of a mystery. Take your child to visit a local planetarium. Experience the wonder that the ancient scholars must have felt. Then go outside and try to discover the constellations for yourself.

Day of the Holy Kings

In Mexico the day of the Holy Kings is January 6 and has been celebrated ever since the Spanish people came to this continent. Christmas decorations are left up until this time. It is on this day that children receive their gifts. A pinata is often used as a party game at this time. Make a pinata and celebrate the journey of the three kings to find baby Jesus.

Supplies: a large brown paper bag, newspaper, masking tape, tempera paint, paintbrushes, crepe paper, wrapped candies, small gifts, party favors, yarn.

Place the candies and small gifts in the bottom of the bag. Stuff the bag with newspaper. Gather the top and wrap with masking tape. Decorate the bag. Cut crepe paper into long streamers and tape to the bag. With yarn or string attach the bag to a tree limb or to a ceiling hook. Take turns using a stick or a broom handle to hit the pinata until it breaks.

ZONE IN
God was made known to all people through Jesus.

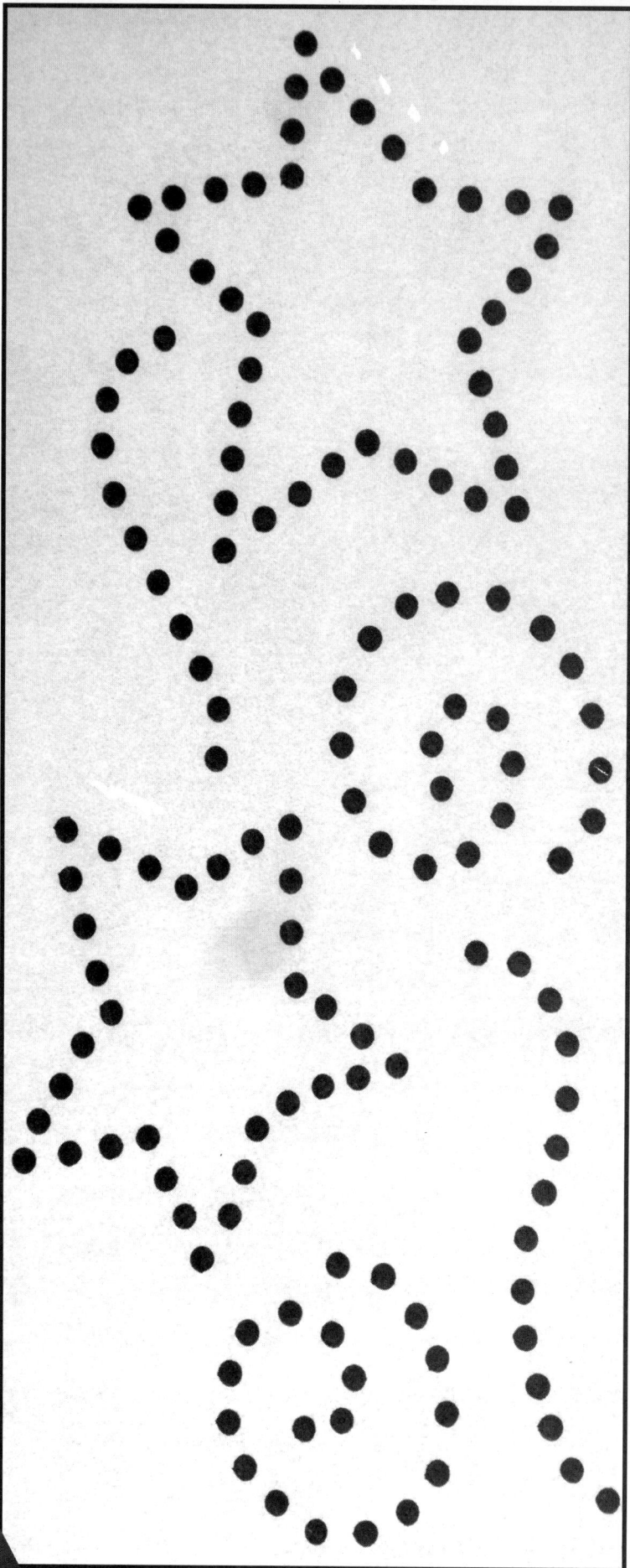

comet

meteor

asteroid

nova

black hole

nebula

star

planet

Reproducible 6A

BIBLEZONE™

Reproducible 6B

81

Talking to God

Enter the Zone™

Bible Verse
Lord, teach us to pray.
Luke 11:1

Bible Story
Matthew 6:9–13; Luke 11:1–4

Jesus was a man of prayer. He continually turned to God for the strength and power to carry out his ministry. Seeing Jesus' dependence on prayer, it is no wonder the disciples asked Jesus to teach them to pray. Jesus proceeded to teach his disciples how to pray, using a prayer we call the Lord's Prayer. In the first three petitions of the prayer, Jesus focused on God's nature, kingdom, and will. In the remaining petitions of the prayer, he focused on human needs --food, forgiveness, and freedom from evil. In providing a prayer on which to model our own prayer life, Jesus offers us a way to practice prayer as both a corporate and a personal spiritual discipline.

Jesus' use of the term *Father* invites all believers to share in a favored relationship to God through Jesus Christ. The Lord's Prayer itself is indicative of the balanced lifestyle that accompanies faithful discipleship. It addresses our relationship to God and others, physical and spiritual needs, and earthly and eternal life. Praying to God is not just something to do when we are in need, feel bad or lost, or are participating in a worship ritual. Jesus taught us to pray with grateful hearts to a loving and forgiving God who guides, encourages, supports, and always cares for each of us.

Learning the Lord's Prayer is a monumental task for many children. It would be detrimental to a child's self-esteem if he or she thought that God's love depended on being able to say the prayer by memory. They can, however, begin to learn the prayer through repetition and activities that involve the words of the prayer. Becoming familiar with the words of the Lord's Prayer allows younger elementary children to participate more fully in worship.

More important to this lesson, however, is the example of Jesus. Not only did Jesus teach his friends to pray, but the children will come to know that Jesus prayed often. Children learn prayer not only from the example of Jesus, but also from examples of the adults in their lives. Pray often for and with the children in your class. Remember that your children come from a variety of backgrounds and some may not have adult models who pray. Consciously look for ways to incorporate prayer into your classroom time.

Jesus teaches us how to talk to God.

Scope the ZONE ™

ZONE	TIME	SUPPLIES	◎ ZILLIES ™
Zoom Into the Zone			
The Great Gate-keeper	10 minutes	chair, blanket or bed-spread, drape	metallic wig, jewel light, foam dice
Stuff It!	5 minutes	recycled newspaper, scissors, trash can or box	prism bag
BibleZone ™			
Weighed Down	10 minutes	recycled newspaper	pom-poms, glitter balls
The Lord's Prayer	5 minutes	none	none
You're On My List	10 minutes	none	none
LifeZone			
Sing and Celebrate	5 minutes	none	kazoos
Pockets O'Prayer	10 minutes	Reproducibles 7A and 7B, crayons or felt-tip markers, scissors, tape, glue, googly eyes (optional)	small pom-poms
Spotlight Prayer	5 minutes	none	jewel light

◎ Zillies ™ are found in the **BibleZone** ™ **FUNspirational** ™ **Kit.**

Zoom Into the Zone™

Choose one or more activities to catch your children's interest.

Supplies:
blanket or bedspread, fabric drape

Zillies™:
metallic wig, jewel light, foam dice

The Great Gatekeeper

Give early arrivals half-sheets of newspaper as they come in. Let them crumple the newspaper into balls and fill a box or trash can with the balls for the next activity. Set a chair in the center of the room. Cover with a blanket or bedspread. Wrap a colorful piece of cloth around the shoulders and wear the **metallic wig**. Walk into the room regally and take a seat in the special chair. Indicate which child comes next by using the **jewel light**.

Say: I am The Great Gatekeeper. All that wish to sit at my feet and learn must first get permission. Form a line here.

Have each child repeat after you: *Oh Great Gatekeeper, may I please take a seat at your feet?* Hand that child one of the foam dice to throw. An even number means the child may take a seat. An odd number means that child must go to the back of the line.

When all the children are seated, ask: Was this a good way of letting you come to the circle? (*It was very formal and took a long time.*) **How did it make you feel?** (*Good if you got to sit down quickly; bad if you had to wait.*)

Say: Long ago in Bible times, talking to God was a lot like this. People had special times when they could pray, and they had special prayers that they could say. But Jesus changed all of that. He taught his people that they could talk with God at any time or any place.

Supplies:
recycled newspaper, scissors, trash can or box

Zillies™:
prism bag

Stuff It!

Say: Let's think about all the different things you do during the day. For everything you do we will put one newspaper ball in this bag.

As each child names an activity, let him or her put a newspaper ball in the bag. Encourage the children to name activities such as getting dressed and eating breakfast. If no one mentions praying, add that to the list. Make sure the bag is totally stuffed before you add it to the list.

Say: There's no room! What should I do with it? (*Invite the children to make suggestions such as: take something else out, or squeeze it really tightly.*)

Ask: How many of you get so busy that sometimes you forget to pray? Is that a good thing to do? Do you think Jesus ever forgot to pray?

Bible ZONE™

Choose one or more activities to immerse your children in the Bible story.

Weighed Down

Supplies:
recycled newspaper

Zillies™:
pom-poms

(D)ivide the children into groups of four or six. If you have a small group, let everyone be in one group. Have the children form a circle and extend their hands. Give each team a sheet of newspaper to hold onto.

Ask: Why do we talk to God? (*We talk to God to say thank you, we talk to God when we're afraid, and we talk to God when we are worried.*) **What would happen if we didn't talk to God?** (*We would keep all those things inside.*) **How would that feel?** (*At first it might not be too bad, but after awhile, it would get very, very heavy.*)

Say: Let's see what would happen if we just let our worries and concerns just pile up. The only rule is that you cannot drop your arms. Let's see which team lasts the longest.

Go around the group and add pom-poms to the newspaper. Each time, talk about things the children could be worried about or afraid of. Do it slowly and methodically. Soon the children will begin to get tired. When they start to complain about their arms hurting, collect all the items.

Say: Each of the items was very light. But the newspaper began to feel heavier and heavier. That's how we would feel if we couldn't talk to God.

ZONE IN™

Jesus teaches us how to talk to God.

The Lord's Prayer

by Sharilyn S. Adair

Ask: When do you pray? Do you pray at bedtime? Do you pray at meals? Do you pray when you get up in the morning? Did you know that in Bible times there were special times when people prayed? Did you know that there were special words they used to pray? Did you know that there were special positions they used to pray?

Say: Prayer was very formal in Bible times. If a person lived in Jerusalem, it was the custom to go to the temple to pray. Those who were not in the holy city would open their windows toward Jerusalem and pray in that direction. The people prayed in the morning at 9 o'clock, at noon, and at 3 o'clock in the afternoon. Sometimes people also prayed at mealtimes. Not only was prayer a good thing to do; it was a duty of the people. Jesus prayed often, but he did not always pray as the religious leaders taught the people.

In the story today we find the prayer that we call The Lord's Prayer. Our church uses this prayer in worship. Today I want you to help me tell the Bible story in a different way. Every time you hear the word pray, we will assume one of the positions used and say: I can talk to God any time, any place, about anything. We will follow the lead of the person to whom I toss the comet ball as to which position we use. The first position is the one that is usually used: standing up, hands outstretched with palms up, looking up. When people were feeling humble, they kneeled down, looked down, and folded their hands in front. When someone was really upset, they lay down on the ground and spread their hands out. Let's practice all three positions. (*Have the children try all three positions. The first was the most often-used position for prayer in Bible times.*)

Jesus led a hectic life. Everywhere he went people followed. People wanted him to bless them, heal them, or teach them. He hardly ever had a moment to himself. So whenever he could, Jesus found time to go off by himself. It was during these times that Jesus would talk to God. In this quiet time, Jesus would **pray**. (*Toss the comet ball to one of the children who will assume a prayer position; the group will copy as they say: I can talk to God any time, any place, about anything.*)

Jesus' disciples noticed that Jesus often went off to be alone when he talked with God. He did not use the formal prayers that they used in the Temple. His praying seemed more natural and friendly than the public prayers they were used to hearing.

So one day one of his disciples said, "John the Baptist taught his followers how to talk to God. We want to talk to God just as you do. Do you say special words? Do you address God in a special way? Jesus, teach us to *pray.*" (*Toss the comet ball to a child.*)

"Do not talk to God as some people do. Their prayers are loud and showy. They shout them from the street corners. They yell them in the Temple. They use many words so that other people who hear them will be impressed with them. That is not how God wants us to *pray.*"

"Those people are more interested in what other people will think than in really talking to God. When you want to talk to God, go off by yourself. God knows what is in your heart before you say a word," Jesus told his friends. "You don't have to use big words or to make long speeches when you *pray.*"

Say: Then Jesus taught his friends a simple way to talk to God. We can learn this prayer together.

Divide the group into pairs. If you have an uneven number, assign one group of three students. After you introduce the first section of the prayer, have partners take turns saying it to each other. Then say it in unison. When you have covered all sections of the prayer in this way, have the total group pray it together.

We talk directly to God, our loving parent. We praise God and say that God is holy: **Our Father who art in heaven, hallowed be thy name.**

We talk about our hope that God will come to rule in the hearts of all people everywhere so that everyone can know God's goodness and love: **Thy kingdom come. Thy will be done, on earth as it is in heaven.**

We ask God for food: **Give us this day our daily bread.**

We ask God's forgiveness for anything we have done wrong or have not done that we should have done, knowing that God expects us to forgive others: **And forgive us our trespasses, as we forgive those who trespass against us.**

We ask for God's help as we make choices and to not give in to our weaknesses and to that which is evil: **Lead us not into temptation, but deliver us from evil.**

Again we praise God as the ruler of all: **For thine is the kingdom, and the power, and the glory, forever. Amen.**

Bible ZONE™

Choose one or more activities to immerse your children in the Bible story.

Supplies:
none

Zillies™:
none

You're on My List

Bring the children together in an open space.

Say: Jesus taught us that we can talk to God about anything at any time or any place. One of the things we can do is pray for each other. When one of us is sick or in trouble we can ask God to help. Sometimes we can just say "thank you" to God for some of our friends. Let's play a game to remind us to pray for one another.

Select one child to be IT. Have the children form a circle with their chairs. As IT walks around the group, he or she will say "I'm praying for" and name one of the children. Each child that IT names must get in line behind IT. Once IT gets a large group (or small group) of followers, then he or she says "Amen."

At this point all the children are to try to get back to their chairs. IT tries to get one of the chairs instead. The child who is left without a chair becomes the next IT.

ZONE IN™

Jesus teaches us how to talk to God.

After the game, remind the children that it is important to pray for one another. If you wish to have prayer partners, let the children write their names on slips of paper and let each child draw a prayer partner for the next week.

Choose one or more activities to bring the Bible to life.

Sing and Celebrate

Supplies:
cassette player

Zillies™:
kazoos, Cassette

(M)ake a copy of the words for each child or make a songchart for the group. Give each child a kazoo. Divide the children and the stanzas into two groups. While one group is singing, the other group is playing the kazoos. Then reverse. This song is sung to the tune of "She'll Be Comin' 'Round the Mountain."

Jesus Told a Story
Oh, Jesus told a story about prayer,
oh, Jesus told a story about prayer.
Take time every day,
to turn to God and pray,
oh, Jesus told a story about prayer.

Oh, God knows what we need before we ask,
oh, God knows what we need before we ask.
Our heart's an open book;
All God has to do is look.
Oh, God knows what we need before we ask.

Oh, we can talk to God anywhere,
oh, we can talk to God anywhere.
No matter where we are
In a plane or in a car,
Oh, we can talk to God anywhere.

Oh, we can talk to God at any time,
oh, we can talk to God at any time.
Morning noon or night
Whether it is dark or light,
Oh, we can talk to God at any time.

Oh, we can bring our troubles straight to God.
Oh, we can bring our troubles straight to God.
Whether they are big or small,
God listens to them all.
Oh, we can bring our troubles straight to God.

Words: Stanza 1 by Jenni Douglas, © 1990 Graded Press; stanzas 2–5 by LeeDell Stickler, © 1998 Abingdon Press.

Life Zone

Choose one or more activities to bring the Bible to life.

Supplies:
Reproducibles 7A and 7B, crayons or felt-tip markers, scissors, tape, glue, googly eyes (optional)

Zillies™:
small pom-poms

Pockets O'Prayer

Give each child a copy of Pockets O'Prayer (*Reproducibles 7A and 7B.*)

Say: **Jesus knew how important it was that we talk to God every day. Jesus didn't want anything to get between us and God. Let's make a prayer reminder.**

Show the children how to cut out and fold Pockets so that he will stand up. Glue one of the small **pom-poms** on the kangaroo for his nose. If you have the googly eyes (optional) let the children glue those on as well. Then cut out the various prayer cards.

Ask: **Who do we need to pray for?** (*persons who are sick, persons who are hungry, persons who lead our country, and so forth*)

Jesus teaches us how to talk to God.

Supplies:
none

Zillies™:
jewel light

Spotlight Prayer

Have the children form a prayer circle on the floor.

Ask: **Isn't it wonderful that we can talk to God at any time and any place about any thing?**

Say: **I am going to pass the light around the circle. When the light comes to you, tell us one thing you want to thank God for. Then we will all say, "Thank you, God."**

Pass the light around the circle. When it gets back to you, **pray:** *Thank you God for all of these boys and girls. I am so glad they are here today. Amen.*

Remind the children to take home Pockets O'Prayer. Make a copy of HomeZone for each family in the group.

Home Zone For Parents

Bible Verse
Lord, teach us to pray.
Luke 11:1

Bible Story
Matthew 6:9–13; Luke 11:1–4

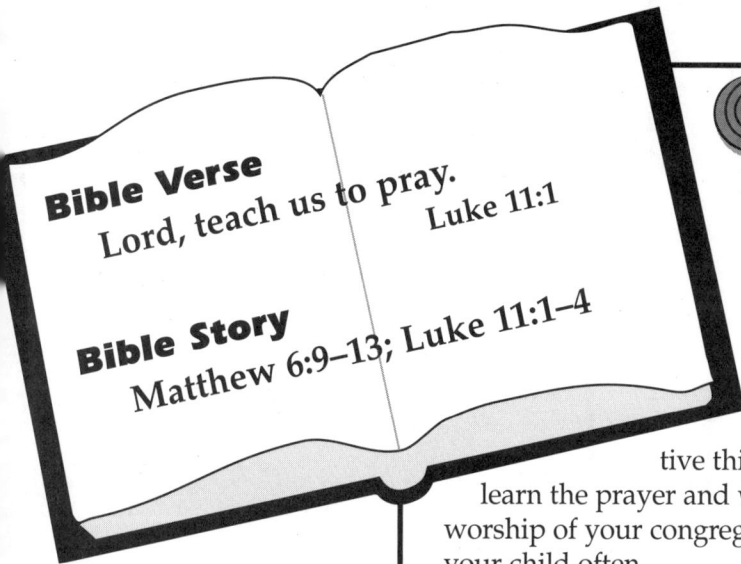

In today's Bible story your child heard how Jesus taught his disciples to pray. From this story, your child also heard the special prayer that Jesus taught his friends. Today we call that prayer the Lord's Prayer. This prayer is used in worship in most churches. Learning the Lord's Prayer is important, but do not put too much pressure on your child to do so. Praying should be an honest and instinctive thing to do. With repetition, your child will learn the prayer and will be able to participate in the corporate worship of your congregation. Set an example of prayer. Pray with your child often.

Praying With Your Child

We can talk to God any time and any place. What an open invitation that is! And yet most people are afraid to pray and feel uncomfortable talking with their children about prayer. Here are some helpful suggestions:

1. Speak to God as though God is a close and treasured friend. What other friend offers us the opportunity for conversation at any time or any place?

2. Keep it simple. Even Jesus taught his friends that God wasn't interested in fancy prayers that mean nothing. Especially when praying with children, short and uncomplicated is best.

3. Pray for persons you know. Let your child see that he or she can turn to God for ordinary things. God is with us in our daily lives and is concerned about us.

4. Pray for persons you may not know but whose actions influence your life. Let your child understand that she or he can be a part of a community of persons who pray.

5. Pray spontaneously. Let your child know that you really do talk to God. Pray when your child is sick. Thank God for a beautiful sunset or a slice or watermelon or a baby kitten....

Help your child remember, however, that prayer is a conversation. Sometimes we have to listen for God's response.

ZONE IN

Jesus teaches us how to talk to God.

1.

Fold Kangaroo in half

Cut slit for pocket

2.

Open out

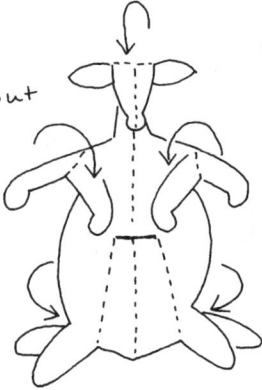

Fold on dashed lines:
* head
* arms
* legs

3. ~Back of Kangaroo~

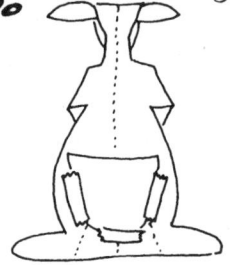

Tape pocket behind slit

4.

Folded Prayers go in the pocket!

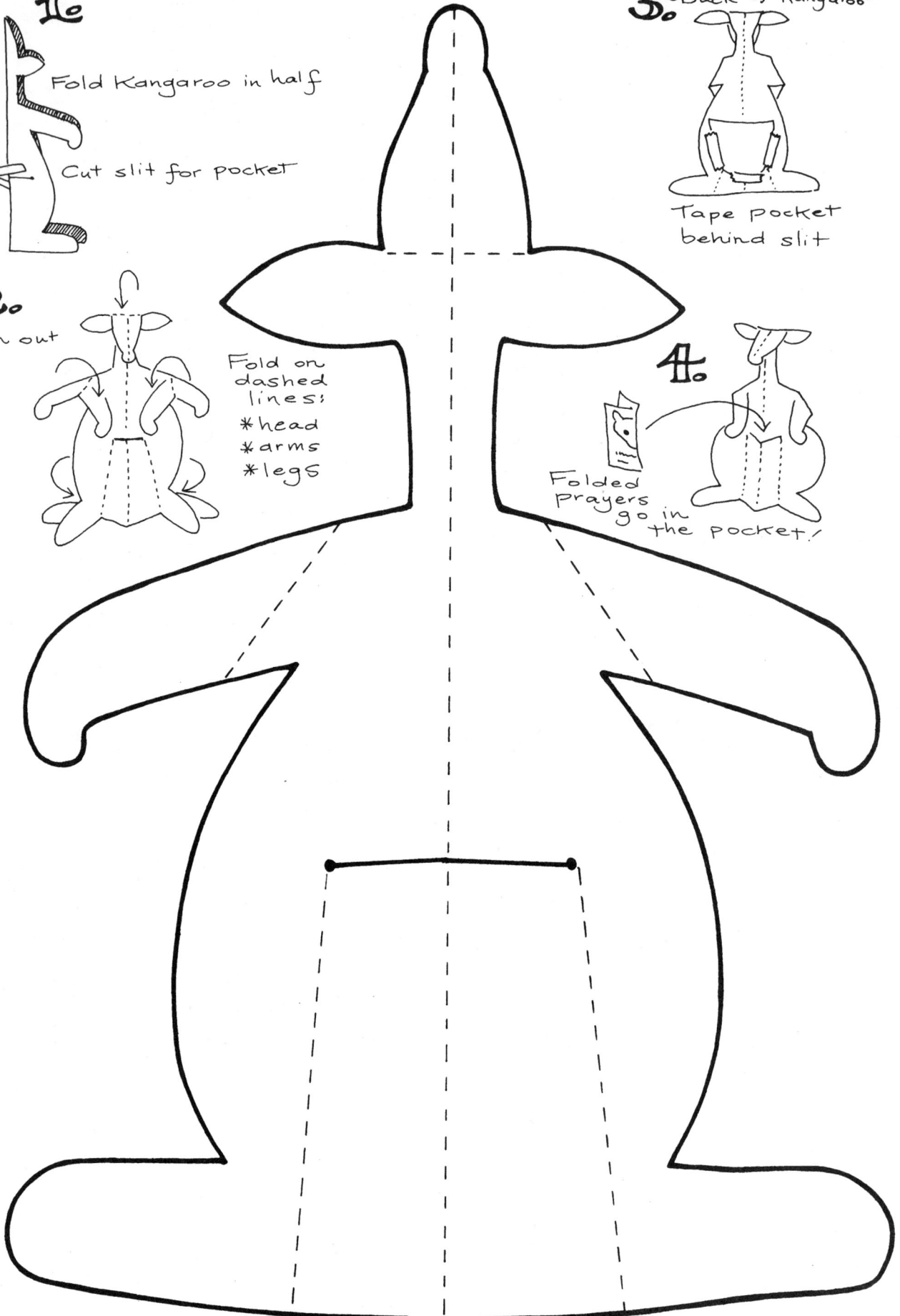

Reproducible 7A

BibleZone™

For those who are sick

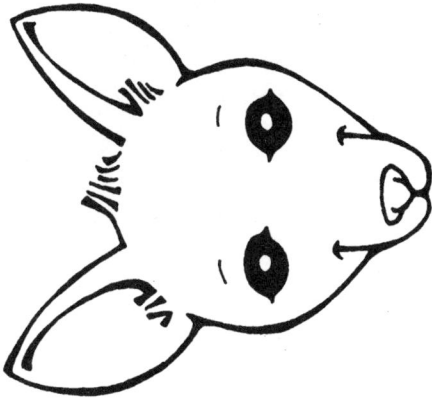

For those who are hungry.

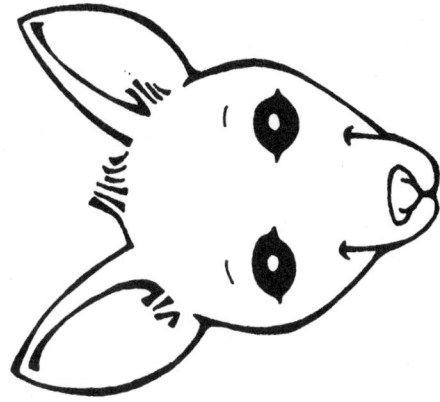

For my friends

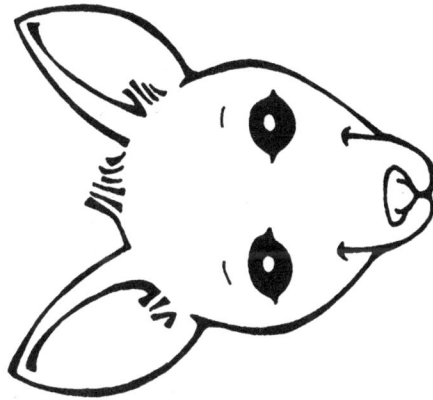

For my family

For those without homes.

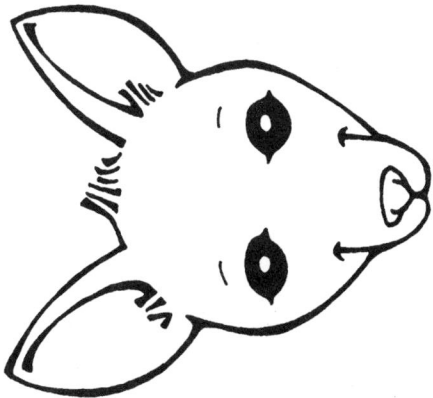

For my church

Reproducible 7B

Beatitude Attitudes

Enter the ZONE™

Bible Verse

Be happy and glad, for a great reward is kept for you in heaven.

Matthew 5:12, *Good News Bible*

Bible Story

Matthew 5:1–12, *Good News Bible*

The Scripture reference for today is a collection of brief blessings and sayings that are more commonly known as The Beatitudes. The Beatitudes are part of a longer text known as the Sermon on the Mount. The Sermon on the Mount is also found in a shorter version in the Book of Luke.

The Sermon on the Mount is thought to sum up the all-around message of Jesus' teachings. The content awakens and strengthens the individual conscience and suggests an example that requires faith and spiritual determination to follow. These powerful and searching sayings left much open for interpretation and are a good illustration of the problematic character of Jesus' teachings.

The Beatitudes, or the first twelve verses, express a paradoxical world. The kingdom of God as explained by Jesus is the reverse of the world as it appears to the average person. These sayings of Jesus forced persons to rethink their most basic reactions. Jesus goes to great lengths to assure the

people that he is not advocating the dissolution of the Law of Moses, but that through his teachings, the Law can be fulfilled. For Jesus, the goal of discipleship, although unattainable, is to be perfect as God is perfect.

Surely a person even today would hear Jesus' words with skepticism. But Jesus knew that his words would shock. The Kingdom of God sets everything upside down from what is expected. Persons usually return aggressive behavior with equally aggressive behavior. Wealth and accumulation of material goods are not only respected, but desired. People who exhibit traits of humility and meekness ar considered weak and easy to take advantage of. Doing what is right should not be a painful experience. So if this is the accustomed reaction, how do we teach such lessons to the children? Just as Jesus did. We model them. We live them. We affirm them when we see them in action. We enable the children to model them too.

ZONE IN

Jesus teaches us how to live so that we can be happy.

Scope the ZONE

ZONE	TIME	SUPPLIES	◎ ZILLIES™
Zoom Into the Zone			
Happiness Is	15 minutes	Reproducibles 8A and 8B, crayons or felt-tip markers, tape or glue, scissors.	none
Frozen Fingers	5 minutes	none	none
BibleZone™			
Are You Happy, Fox?	10 minutes	masking tape	none
A Beatitude Attitude Rap	5 minutes	none	none
Happiness Gran Prix	10 minutes	tape, Reproducible 8A (bottom), masking tape, construction paper, scissors	friction cars
LifeZone			
Sing and Celebrate	5 minutes	cassette	Cassette
Happiness Fling	5 minutes	Flingers (Reproducible 8B)	none
Happy Hand Talk	5 minutes	none	glitter balls

◎ Zillies™ are found in the **BibleZone™ FUNspirational™ Kit.**

Zoom Into the ⊚ᴢᴼᴺᴱ™

Choose one or more activities to catch your children's interest.

Supplies:
Reproducibles 8A
and 8B, crayons
or felt-tip mark-
ers, tape or
glue, scissors.

Zillies™:
none

Happiness Is. . .

(M)ake a copy of Happiness Is . . . *(Reproducible 8A)* for each child in the group. As the children arrive, greet them warmly and hand out the activity.

Ask: What is happiness? Is it something you have or something that will happen? Is it a way of living or a person?

Have the children draw a picture of what they think happiness is. After the children have drawn their picture, let them assemble their Flingers *(Reproducible 8B)*. Color the flinger tube and the flinger keys. Show the children how to roll the two parts and make tubes—one long and narrow, the other short and wider. Make sure the flinger keys will fit over the flinger tube. Set these aside for later in the lesson.

Supplies:
none

Zillies™:
none

Frozen Fingers

(B)ring the children together in a circle in the storytelling area.

Then ask: Have you ever had someone teach you something special? How did you feel knowing this and knowing that no one else did? Did it make you feel special? Were you anxious to share this with someone else?

Say: Let me share a special hand trick that you can do and share with a friend. First, put your hands together, the fingers and thumb of the right hand touching the fingers and thumb of the left hand. Move the palms apart while keeping the fingers together. Then bend the middle finger down, so that the knuckle of the right middle finger is touching the knuckle of the left middle finger. Now I want you to tap your index fingers against each other. (*Wait as the children tap their fingers.*) **Tap your pinky fingers against each other.** (*Wait while the children tap their pinky fingers.*) **Now tap your ring fingers together.** (*Wait while the children struggle to accomplish this task.*)

Ask: What's the matter? Can't you do it?

Say: This will be a fun thing to share with your friends. In today's Bible story Jesus shares something special with his friends. It's not a trick like I shared with you, but it is a key to living so that you will be happy. Wouldn't that be a great thing to know! (*Let the children share their happiness pictures.*)

Bible Z⦿NE™

Choose one or more activities to immerse your children in the Bible story.

Are You Happy, Fox?

Supplies:
masking tape

Zillies™:
none

Have the children come to an open area of the room. Create a safety zone at one end of the room and the Fox's Den at the other end of the room. Have all the children but one stand in the safety zone. Select one child to be Fox. Have Fox stand in the den facing away from the safety zone. The object of the game is for the children to see how close they can get to Fox before he turns around and catches them.

The players will take steps out of the safety zone toward the fox. Each time the group will ask: Are you happy, Fox? Fox will answer, "No, I'm sad," or "No, I'm tired," or "No, I'm angry." If Fox answers, "Yes, I'm happy", then Fox turns around and tries to catch the children before they get back to the safety zone.

When the game is over, bring the children back to the storytelling area.

Say: Everyone wants to be happy. But there are just times when we don't feel happy. Jesus knew this. But he also knew that God wants us to be happy and that when we are with God we will always be happy.

ZONE IN™ Jesus teaches us how to live so that we can be happy.

Ask: Can you walk happy? What does a happy walk look like? What does a sad walk look like? How do you walk when you're angry? How do you walk when your tired? How do you walk when you're scared? (Pause after each question and give the children an opportunity to imitate the feelings in their walks.)

The Beatitude Attitude Rap

by LeeDell Stickler

Say: today's Scripture lesson is done in the form of a rap. The chorus can be done by everyone I will read the verses. After we've done it once, then we can try it all together.

Let the children suggest movements to go with the chorus. You may want to do a push slide to the right two times, then do a push slide to the left two times and continue repeating to the rhythm.

> **Uh, huh. That's right!**
> **What Jesus said is true.**
> **I've got the Beatitude Attitude**
> **And I know just what to do.**

Jesus gathered his friends together
To teach them just how they should live
And how they should treat one another
How to love and how to forgive.

Chorus:
Uh, huh. That's right!
What Jesus said is true.
I've got the Beatitude Attitude
And I know just what to do.

One day as they sat on a mountain
Jesus spoke to the people so true,
"Folks, if you want to be happy,
Then this is just what you should do."

Chorus:

"If your feelin' real down in the dumps now,
Thinkin' all of the good things are past.
Just remember God knows whats inside you
And will give you some comfort at last.

Chorus:

For you people whose spirits are heavy,
Don't feel like your life's in a mess.
Take heart for God's made you a promise.
God's kingdom is yours, nothin' less.

Chorus:

If your so humble you can't lift your
eyes up
Or so shy you'll fall over at "boo!"
God won't overlook you, I promise.
God's wonderful earth is for you.

Chorus:

For those who show others mercy,
You'll find mercy in all that you do.
And for those who possess a pure
heart
God's face will be open to you.

Chorus:

If you're thinkin' your life is a.trial
And nothing seems just as it should,
Rejoice and remember God's
promise.
Soon your life will be better than
good.

Chorus:

When you come to the end of
life's journey
And all of your pathways are trod,
Just remember the words that I'm
saying
And you'll be called the children of
God.

Teach the children the sign language for the
phrase: For I am called a child of God.

For   I   am called

a child of God

Bible Zone™

Choose one or more activities to immerse your children in the Bible story.

Supplies:
Reproducible 8A (bottom), tape, masking tape, construction paper, scissors

Zillies™:
friction cars

Happiness Gran Prix

Make a two copies of the Beatitudes *(Reproducible 8A [bottom])*. Clear an open area in the center of the room.

Have the children count off by twos. All the ones will be on Team A. All the twos will be on Team B. Put a masking tape line across the center of the playing area. Walk six feet back from the line and put another masking tape line. This is the starting line. Then from the center point, walk three feet in the other direction. Put a third masking tape line. This is the PIT.

Each team will select two members to be the PIT crew, one person to be the Keeper, and the remainder will be the drivers (up to eight children).

PIT Crew (two children): Catch the racing car, attach the Beatitude to the top with tape and send it back to the starting point.
Keepers (one or two children): Take the Beatitude from the top of the car and tape it onto construction paper.
Drivers (whoever is left): Stand behind the starting line and send the car toward the PIT.

Give the teams time to decide who will be PIT crew and who will be the Drivers and the Keepers. Have the Drivers line up single file behind the starting line. Give the first driver in each line the racing car. As the leader says "Go!" each Driver will launch the team car toward the PIT. The car must pass the center line in order for a PIT crew member to retrieve it. If it doesn't go across, the driver must go and get it and try again.

Once the race car has crossed the middle line, the PIT crew retrieves the car, tapes one of the Beatitudes to the top and sends it back. The Keepers remove the square of paper and give the car to the next driver in line. The game continues until all the Beatitudes have been ferried across the racing zone. The first team to get all the Beatitudes together wins the relay.

Remind the children that the Beatitudes are special actions and attitudes that Jesus taught his disciples that would bring true happiness.

Jesus teaches us how to live so that we can be happy.

Choose one or more activities to bring the Bible to life.

Sing and Celebrate

Supplies:
cassette player

Zillies™:
Cassette

Assign the different roles to small groups of children. Select one child to present a blanket to the woman and a glass of water to the man.

The Blessing
Woman who is cold (REFRAIN 1):
Bless you, my child, for you have been a blessing.
May the good Lord smile down upon you this day,
for you gave me kindness when I was in need.
God bless you, my child, as you have blessed me.

Group (REFRAIN 2):
Bless you, my child, for you have been a blessing.
May the good Lord smile down upon you this day,
for you gave her kindness when she was in need.
(Woman)
God bless you, my child, as you have blessed me.

Thirsty Man:
REFRAIN 1

Woman and Man :
You shared a part of you, the heart of who you are.
You did not know me, yet you showed me love.

Group:
Bless you, my child, for you have been a blessing.
May the good Lord smile down upon you this day,
for you gave me kindness when I was in need.
for you gave them kindness when they were in need.

Thirsty Man:
God bless you, my child, as you have blessed me.

Life Zone

Choose one or more activities to bring the Bible to life.

Supplies:
Flingers and Keys
to Happiness
(Reproducible
8B)

Zillies™:
none

Happiness Fling

Have the children get their flingers and their keys to happiness (Reproducible 8B) that they made earlier in the lesson.

Say: **Jesus taught his friends certain actions and attitudes. If his friends would keep theses in mind, they would be the keys to true happiness.**

Bring everyone to one side of the room. Have them slip their keys to happiness over the flinger tube. Then show them how to "fling" the keys to happiness into the world.

Say: **Whenever anyone thinks of a Beatitude that we talked about today, shout it out. Then we'll all repeat it and fling our keys to happiness. The Beatitudes are attitudes and actions that will help us be happy as well.**

Jesus teaches us how to live so that we can be happy.

Supplies:
none

Zillies™:
none

Happy Hand Talk

Recall the hand signs for the phrase, "For I am called a child of God." Have the children form a circle on the floor or standing up.

Say: **I will say a phrase and after each phrase, I want you to repeat the sign language. Sometimes I feel all alone, but I know God cares about me.** (*Pause.*) **Sometimes I may be sad, but I know God is with me.** (*Pause.*) **I want to live as God intends, and I know God will help me.** (*Pause.*) **I will show mercy to persons.** (*Pause.*) **I will try to keep a pure heart.** (*Pause.*) **I will be a peacemaker.** (*Pause.*) **I will stand up for Jesus no matter what the cost.** (*Pause.*) **Amen.**

Make a copy of HomeZone™ for each family in your class.

Bible Verse
Be happy and glad, for a great reward is kept for you in heaven.
Matthew 5:12, Good News Bible

Bible Story
Matthew 5:1–12, Good News Bible

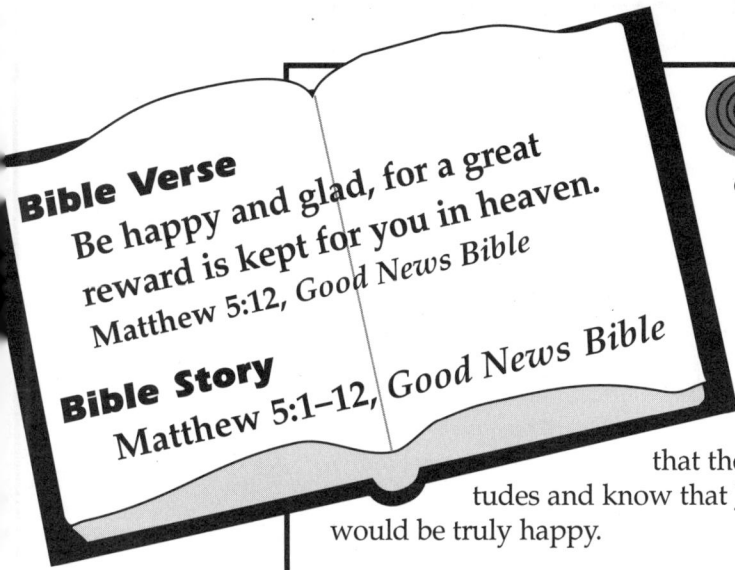

In today's lesson your child learned about a special set of Jesus' teachings called the Beatitudes. The Beatitudes are the first twelve verses of that Scripture often called the Sermon on the Mount. These teachings at first appeared to be a topsy turvy version of what the people had always been taught to believe. Where most of these teachings are beyond the conceptual level of young it is enough that they become familiar with the name Beatitudes and know that Jesus tried to teach people how to that they would be truly happy.

Happiness Is

Today we asked your child to draw a picture of what he or she thought happiness was. Invite him or her to share this picture with you. Talk about what makes people truly happy. Too many times happiness is equated with the accumulation of things. In the Bible Jesus teaches his friends how to have true happiness.

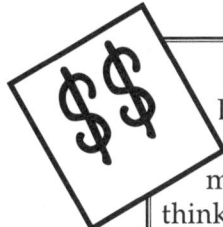

Free Fun!

$$ Look for ways to share outings and activities that don't cost very much money. Many of our children cannot think of any way to have fun that doesn't cost money. Make it a family task to one weekend a month to do fun things that are free or at least very inexpensive. Some suggestions might be:

1. Cook together as a family. Pick one meal and everyone have a part.
2. Play games together. Let each person have a favorite game and the rest of the family participate.
3. Go on a winter time picnic. Most people relegate picnics to the summer. Think how interesting the woods or the parks look in the winter. Take hot chocolate and a favorite soup to go along with the sandwiches. Take sports equipment for family games. $$

Jesus teaches us how to live so that we can be happy.

Happiness is. . .

Happy are those who are sad now, because God will comfort them.	Happy are the peacemakers for they will be called children of God.	Happy are the humble for the earth is theirs.	Happy are those who are spiritually poor, for the kingdom of heaven belongs to them.
Happy are the seekers after righteousness, for they shall find it.	Happy are those who show mercy, for mercy will be shown to them.	Happy are the pure in heart for they shall see God.	Happy are those who stand up for Jesus no matter what the cost.

Reproducible 8A

BibleZone™

I've got a Beatitude attitude!

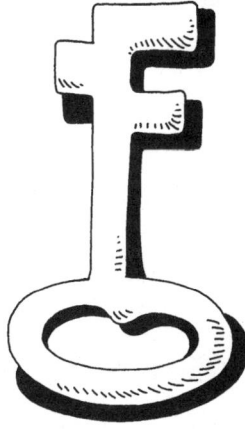

Key to Happiness

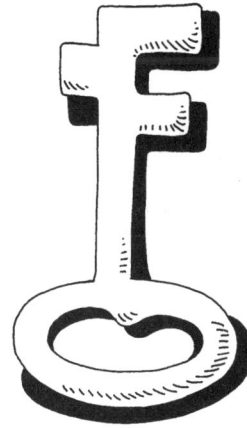

Key to Happiness

Reproducible 8B

The Great Commandment

Enter the **Zone**™

Bible Verse

Love the Lord your God with all your heart,
love your neighbor as yourself.

Matthew 22:37, 39, adapted

Bible Story

Matthew 22:34–40

In the Great Commandments in Matthew 22:35-40, Jesus combined Deuteronomy 6:5, called the Shema, and Leviticus 19:18b. Jesus' answer, as so often happened, came in response to the question from a Pharisaic lawyer who was trying to test Jesus. "Teacher," he asked, "which commandment in the law is greatest?"

The question of which was the greatest commandment seems to have been raised often by the rabbis. The content of Jesus' answer was not new—what was new was how he redefined how we should love God. Love for God manifests itself not only in following the law, but in expanding our love to others. If we love God, we will love our neighbors; when we show love to our neighbors, we are also showing love to God.

The children you teach should experience love through faithful and caring relationships with their parents, family members, teachers, and caregivers. It is important to explain love to children with specific examples of the ways that we can show love.

Young children also need the love for self that Jesus describes as the measure of loving actions toward others. Ironically, their self-love is learned from love shown by significant adults in their worlds. Their self-image is determined largely by messages they receive about themselves early in life. These messages will have a long-lasting impact on each child's ability to give and receive love. Each time you teach, think of specific ways that you can share God's love with your children.

ZONE IN

Jesus teaches us to love God and love one another.

Scope the ZONE

ZONE	TIME	SUPPLIES	ZILLIES™
Zoom Into the Zone			
Copy Cat Hearts	10 minutes	Reproducible 9A, crayons or felt-tip markers	none
Who Do You Love?	5 minutes	none	jewel light
BibleZone™			
Yes–No–Maybe So	10 minutes	none	none
The Case of the Tricky Question	10 minutes	none	jewel light
Body Parts	5 minutes	Reproducible 9B, scissors, masking tape, basket	none
Who's My Neighbor?	5 minutes	none	none
LifeZone			
Sing and Celebrate	5 minutes	cassette player	Cassette
Sign Along Verse	5 minutes	none	none

Zillies™ are found in the **BibleZone™ FUNspirational™ Kit.**

Zoom Into the Zone™

Choose one or more activities to catch your children's interest.

Supplies:
Reproducible 9A,
crayons or felt-
tip markers

Zillies™;
none

Copy Cat Hearts

Make a copy of the half hearts (Reproducible 9A) for each child in the group. Set out crayons and felt-tip markers.

Greet the children as they come in. Try to say something personal to each child.

Say: **Today's Bible lesson is about love. Of course, we all recognize the heart as a symbol of love. On the sheet you have are several hearts of different sizes and designs. But they are only half colored. I want you to make the design on one side match the design on the other side. Then color both sides.**

> **ZONE IN™** **Jesus teaches us to love God and to love one another.**

Supplies:
none

Zillies™;
comet ball

Who Do You Love?

Bring the children together in a circle. They can sit on the floor or sit in chairs.

Say: **Our Bible verse for today tells us to love God and to love one another. Let's play a game called "Who Do You Love?" I will call on someone to begin by tossing the comet ball to them. That person will begin to describe someone in the group that she or he loves. When the person who is being described recognizes himself or herself, that person jumps up and says "That's Me!" If that child is correct, then the person doing the describing tosses the ball to the child who answered correctly and she or he becomes the describer.**

Toss the comet ball to one of the children and **ask: Who do you love?**

Play the game until every child has a turn or until the children begin to get bored.

Bible ZONE ™

Choose one or more activities to immerse your children in the Bible story.

Yes-No-Maybe So

Supplies:
none

Zillies™:
none

S ay: In today's Bible story, some very important people try to trick Jesus into saying something that might get him into trouble. They wanted to get him in trouble because they wanted an excuse to get rid of him, since Jesus was teaching some things that they didn't approve of. Let's play a game where there are certain things we cannot say or we'll get into trouble.

Divide the room in half with an imaginary boundary line. Separate the group into three teams, each standing in line—one player behind the other—on one side of the boundary line.

Say: I am going to take turns asking each of you questions. The person I call on must answer immediately, without hesitation. However, none of you can use the words YES, NO, or MAYBE. If you use one of those words you will go to the end of the line. Players who answer successfully are allowed to cross the boundary into the safety zone.

You may begin with this list of questions and add some of your own. Remember to play fast enough to confuse the players. The first team to get all of its players across to the safety zone is the winner.

1. Are you six years old? (*eight years old, ten years old, seven years old*)
2. Do you like hamburgers? (*hot dogs, pizza, ice cream*)
3. Do you like to do homework?
4. Do you have red pajamas?
5. Can you ride a bicycle?
6. Do you have twenty toes?
7. Is your hair green?
8. Can a dog bark?
9. Does a cat go "squeak, squeak?"
10. Is the sky blue?
11. Does it ever rain on Saturday?
12. Do ice cream cones grow on trees?
13. Do you like weekends?

Move quickly from team to team asking the questions.

After the game is over, **ask: Was it difficult not to say those special words? Do you think Jesus had to be careful about what he said?**

The Case of the Tricky Question

by LeeDell Stickler

Say: Jesus' teachings were very different from what the people were used to hearing from the religious authorities of the day. Some people liked what he had to say. Some wondered by whose authority he spoke. Others thought him a troublemaker and wanted to get rid of him. These people were afraid that Jesus would upset the way things had been and cause them trouble. Many times the religious leaders would try to trick Jesus into saying something wrong. Then they could have him arrested. Today we are going to pretend that Jesus is being tried for teaching against the Law of Moses. Anyone who spoke against the Law of Moses was committing a terrible crime. Let's see what happens.

Characters: Judge Noitawl, Jesus, Prosecutor, Citizen, Defense Council, Court Clerk

Court Clerk: Court is now in session. The honorable Judge Noitawl presiding.

Judge Noitawl: Would the defendant please stand (*Jesus stands.*) You have been charged with speaking against the Law of Moses. How do you plead?

Defense Council: (*Standing*) Not guilty, your honor.

Judge Noitawl: District Attorney, you may call your first witness.

Prosecutor: I would like to call Citizen to the stand.

Defense Council: I object, your honor. The religious leaders set Jesus up. This person was planted just to get him into trouble.

Judge Noitawl: Overruled.

Court Clerk: (*Holds out Bible. Citizen places left hand on Bible and holds up right hand.*) Do you swear that the testimony you are about to give is the truth, the whole truth, and nothing but the truth, so help you God?

Citizen: I do.

Court Clerk: Please state your name.

Citizen: I am Citizen.

Prosecutor: Where were you yesterday afternoon?

Citizen: I had come to the Temple to pray when I saw a crowd gathered. This man was in the center teaching.

Prosecutor: And can you describe what happened next?

Citizen: Jesus had been answering all kinds of questions. He had been very good at dodging all the answers. So I decided to try to trick him.

Defense Council: Objection. You see, your honor, he was being set up. It was a fix.

Judge Noitawl: Overruled. Please continue.

Citizen: I asked Jesus the question "What is the greatest commandment?" If he picked one, then he would be speaking against the Law of Moses.

Defense Council: Objection! That's a trick question! If he answers it, he's in trouble. If he doesn't answer it, he's in trouble.

Judge Noitawl: Objection overruled.

Prosecutor: And what did Jesus answer?

Judge Noitawl: Answer the question, please.

Citizen: He said to "Love the Lord your God with all your heart, with all your soul, and with all your mind.." He said that this was the greatest and most important commandment. Then, Jesus said that the second most important commandment was to love your neighbor as you love yourself.

Prosecutor: Your witness.

Defense Council: And is this a false statement?

Citizen: No. The whole Law of Moses and the teachings of the prophets can be summed up in these two commandments.

Defense Council: So he didn't speak against the Law. (*Turns to judge.*) Your honor, I move that the case be dismissed. There is no evidence against my client.

Judge Noitawl: Prosecutor, do you have any more evidence against this man?

Prosecutor: No, your honor.

Judge Noitawl: (*Pounds gavel.*) This man is innocent. Case dismissed.

Bible Zone™

Choose one or more activities to immerse your children in the Bible story.

Supplies:
Reproducible 9B,
scissors

Zillies™:
none

Body Parts

Make copies of the body parts *(Reproducible 9B)* so that there are enough parts that each child in the group will have one. If you have a small class, then IT will have to name two body parts to make the game more fun. Cut apart the squares, fold and place the body parts in a basket.

Bring the children together in an open space. Form a circle. Let each child choose a body part from the basket.

Say: I am going to choose one of you to be IT. IT will stand in the center of the circle. He or she will say: "Love the Lord your God with all your " and will then name one of the body parts that is pictured on page 117. If the class is small and there are no duplicates, IT should name two body parts. Whoever has that body part must change places in the circle with another person who has that body part. While the two body parts are trying to trade places, IT is trying to tag one of them. Whoever is tagged becomes IT and IT assumes that body part. If IT says: "Love the Lord your God with all your *heart*", then everyone must change places. Whoever is tagged becomes IT in the next game.

Play until everyone has had a chance to be IT or until the children begin to get bored.

Supplies:
none

Zillies™:
none

Who's My Neighbor?

Say: Not only did Jesus tell us that we should love God with our whole hearts and minds, but he also said that we should love our neighbors as ourselves. But who are our neighbors? Let's play a game and see if we can find out for ourselves.

Select on person to be IT. It is blindfolded and stands in the center. When IT says "Go" all the children switch places. When IT says "Stop!" the children freeze immediately. IT then points in any direction. The person pointed to comes forward and stands in front of IT. IT says "Howdy, neighbor." The player who is standing in front of IT must say "Howdy." This can be repeated three times only. If IT guesses the player's identity, then the two change places. If the guess is wrong, the person picked returns to the circle and the one who is IT selects a new player.

Say: It's fun to be good neighbors.

Choose one or more activities to bring the Bible to life.

Sing and Celebrate

Supplies:
cassette player

Zillies™:
Cassette

(M) ake a copy of the words for each child or create a class song chart. Use these motions for the words as you sing:

Whole (*Extend arms out from body, palms up.*); **heart** (*Trace a heart on the chest with index fingers.*); **praise** (*Fold hands as though in prayer.*); **love** (*Cross arms over chest.*); **mind** (*Touch index fingers to right and left temples.*); **hear** (*Touch ears with index fingers.*); **life** (*Extend arms and turn all the way around.*)

With My Whole Heart

With my whole heart,
Lord, let me love You
with my whole heart,
None above You.
Praise and love You
with my whole heart.

With my whole heart,
Lord, let me hear You
with my whole heart.
Ever near you.
Help me hear You
with my whole heart.

With my whole mind,
Lord, let me love You
with my whole mind,
None above You.
Praise and love You
with my whole mind.

With my whole mind,
Lord, let me hear You
with my whole mind,
Ever near You.
Help me hear You
with my whole mind.

With my whole life,
Lord, let me love You
with my whole life,
None above You.
Praise and love You
with my whole life.

With my whole life,
Lord, let me hear You
with my whole life,
Ever near You.
Help me hear You
with my whole life.

ZONE IN™ **Jesus teaches us to love God and also to love one another.**

Life Zone™

Choose one or more activities to bring the Bible to life.

Supplies:
none

Zillies™:
none

Sign Along Verse

Teach the children the American Sign Language gestures for the Bible verse for today, as follows:

Love—Fold the fingers into a fist, thumb across the fingers. Cross at the wrist and press to the heart.

God—Extend the index finger and fold the remaining fingers down, holding them with the thumb. Point this hand forward in front of you; draw it up and then back down. As you bring it down, open the palm, which is facing left.

with—Fold all the fingers down, thumb on the outside of the index fingers. Place the two hands together.

all—The left open hand faces the body. Make a circle with the right hand going out and around the left hand, ending with the back of the right hand in the palm of the left hand.

your—Face the palm out, directing it forward.

heart—Trace a heart on the chest with index fingers.

Play a game as you learn this verse by passing each sign around the circle from one child to another.

Then bring the children together in a prayer circle. **Pray: Dear God, help us to love you with our whole heart. Help us to love our neighbors as we love ourselves. Amen.**

Bible Verse
Love the Lord your God with all your heart, love your neighbor as yourself.

Matthew 22:37, 39, adapted

Bible Story
Matthew 22:34–40

In today's Bible story, your child heard about a Scripture often called the Great Commandment. While the man in the crowd who asked the question "What is the greatest commandment?" was only trying to trick Jesus, Jesus' answer called him up short. Jesus' response summed up all the laws of Moses as well as those of the prophets. Consider: If we love God and love our neighbors, then following the Ten Commandments is a natural thing to do. Help your child learn to be open and accepting of those around him or her and to love God with a whole heart.

Learn to Sign

Children love to use American Sign Language. They are intrigued that persons can actually use their hands to communicate. In today's lesson, your child not only sang the Bible verse but learned to sign the verse as well. Here are the signs your child learned. Practice them yourself and sign the Bible verse together.

Love—Fold the fingers into a fist, with the thumb across the fingers. Cross at the wrist and press to the heart.

God—Extend the index finger and fold the remaining fingers down, holding them with the thumb. Point this hand forward in front of you, draw it up and then back down. As you bring it down, open the palm, which is facing left.

with—Fold all the fingers down, with the thumb on the outside of the index fingers. Place the two hands together.

all—The left open hands face the body. Make a circle with the right hand going out and around the left hand, ending with the back of the right hand in the palm of the left hand.

your—Face the palm out, directing it forward.

heart—Trace a heart on the chest with your index fingers.

Love God with all your heart

Jesus teaches us to love God and to love one another.

With My Whole Heart

Reproducible 9A

BIBLEZONE™

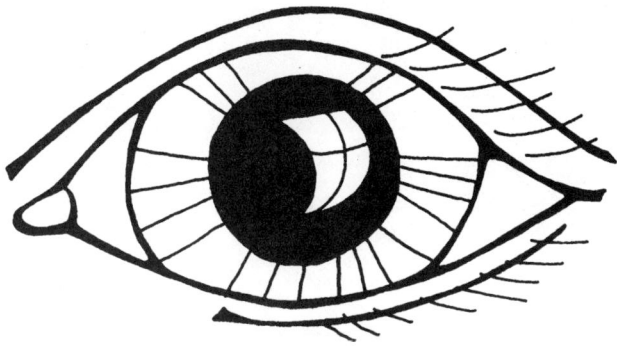
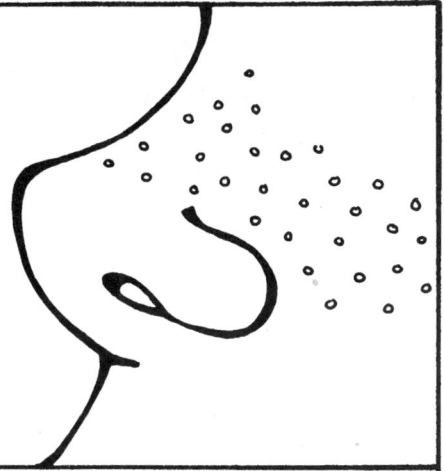

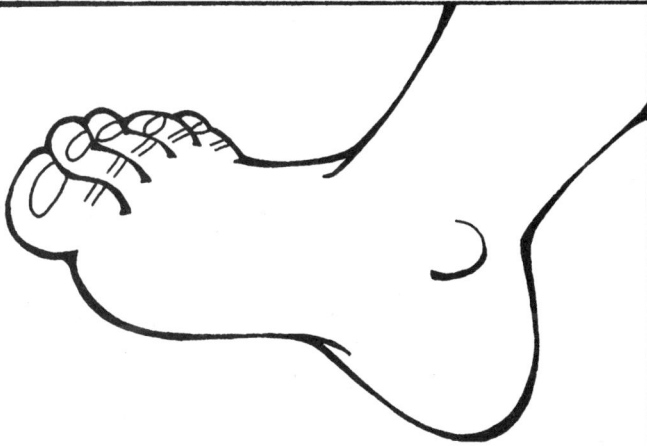
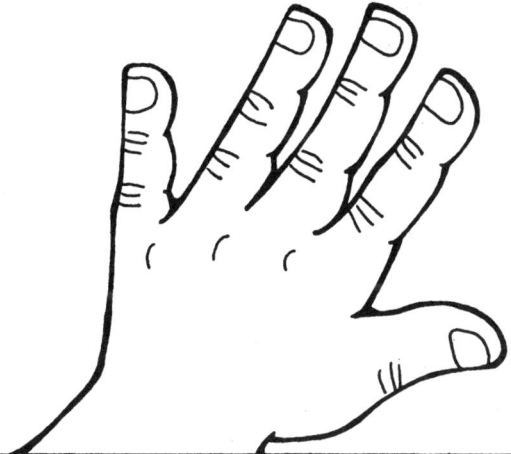
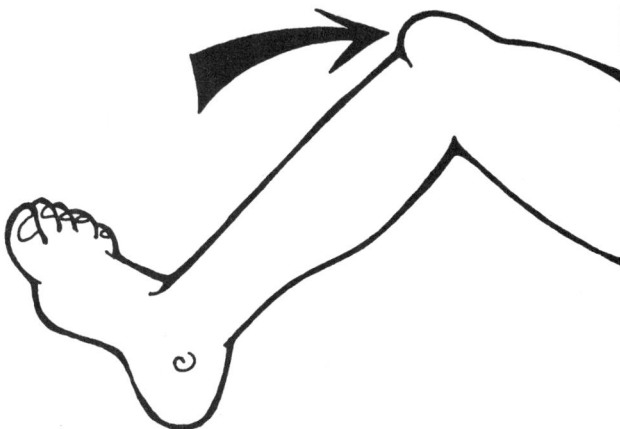
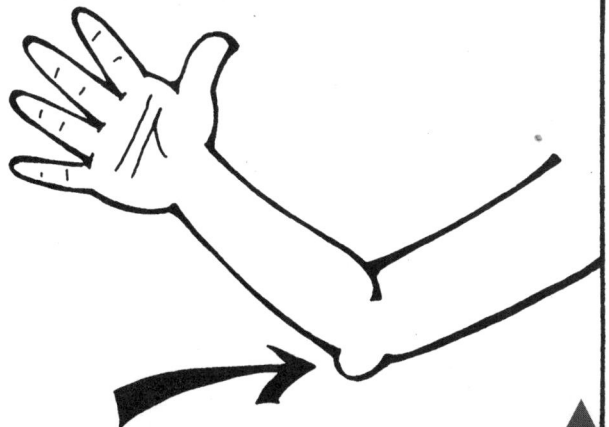

Reproducible 9B

Forgiveness

Enter the Zone™

Bible Verse
Forgive one another.

Ephesians 4:32, *Good News Bible*

Bible Story
Matthew 18:21–35

Jesus had been telling his followers how they should act toward other believers and toward those in the world. As so often happened, Peter, acting as spokesperson for the disciples, came to him with a question. Peter wanted Jesus to rule on the number of times one must forgive a person who has committed a wrong.

In the pre-Israelite period, vengeance toward one who had done wrong had no limits. Among the Jews of Jesus' day the number of times one forgave varied, with three being the fixed number at one place, and seven in another. Peter no doubt knew both of these statements, and believed himself to be most generous when he offered to forgive seven times.

But Jesus says no. As God's mercy toward us has no limits, so our forgiveness toward others must also be limitless. Seventy times seven (or as some translations state, seventy-seven) means that our mercy toward others must have no end.

Younger elementary children are more and more frequently finding themselves in arenas with other children. Each situation demands that there be a certain amount of give and take as well as cooperation. But on the whole, children at this age are less self-centered and look for agreeable solutions to conflict. Children want to be a part of the group. Being disagreeable often means being left out of an activity or a social interaction.

However, watch for children who do not stand up for themselves and are frequently doormats because they subjugate their needs to the needs of all others. Let the children work out their own disagreements unless physical violence seems imminent. Encourage the children to forgive and to seek forgiveness when they do wrong. Remind them, however, that when we are sorry we try very hard not to repeat the offending act.

Jesus teaches us to forgive one another.

Scope the ZONE ™

ZONE	TIME	SUPPLIES	☉ ZILLIES ™
Zoom Into the Zone			
Make Story Puppets	10 minutes	Reproducibles 10A and 10B, crayons or felt-tip markers, construction paper, tape (Optional: wooden paint stirrer or ruler)	none
Forbidden Sevens	5 minutes	none	construction paper, kazoos
BibleZone ™			
Please, Kind Person	10 minutes	none	metallic wig
The Unforgiving Servant	10 minutes	story puppets	none
Break the Circle	10 minutes	none	none
LifeZone			
Sing and Celebrate	5 minutes	cassette player	Cassette, kazoos
Think Fast	5 minutes	none	comet ball
Happy Hands	5 minutes	none	none

☉ Zillies™ are found in the **BibleZone™ FUNspirational™ Kit.**

Choose one or more activities to catch your children's interest.

Supplies:
Reproducibles 10A and 10B, crayons or felt-tip markers, construction paper, tape (Optional: wooden paint stirrer or ruler)

Zillies™:
none

Make Story Puppets

Make a set of the story puppets *(Reproducibles 10A and 10B)* for each group of four children. Cut strips of construction paper one inch wide and six inches long. These will be the handles for the puppets.

Greet the children as they come in. Assign each child to a story team (four to a team) and let each child color and assemble a story puppet. (Once the puppet is colored, attach the handle to the back of the puppet. If you prefer, use a wooden paint stirrer or a ruler instead of the handles.)

Say: Today we are going to perform a Bible story for each team. There are four characters in the story. When you finish, leave your puppet in the story area and come to the circle.

ZONE IN™ Jesus teaches us to forgive one another.

Supplies:
none

Zillies™:
kazoos

Forbidden Sevens

Bring the children together in a circle on the floor or in chairs. This game is a counting game which seems simple enough, except when it comes to sevens. Seven is the forbidden number.

Say: In today's Bible story, the number seven plays an important role. Jesus tells Peter he is supposed to do something not seven times but seventy times seven times. Let's play a game.

Have the children stand in a circle ready to count off. Any time a seven shows up —7, 17, 27, 37, 47, and so forth, the number is replaced by humming into the kazoo. For example, 1–2–3–4–5–6–(hum)–8–9–10–11–12–13–14–15–16–(hum). The object of the game is to get to 100 without making a mistake. If one person forgets to hum into his or her kazoo, then everyone has to go back to the beginning and start over. If you have an older group of children, you may want to add multiples of seven as well. Play until the group reaches 100 or the children begin to get bored.

Say: In Bible times the number seven stood for perfection. God created the world in six days and rested on the seventh. Farmers were supposed to plow the land for six years and let it rest on the seventh.

Bible ZONE™

Choose one or more activities to immerse your children in the Bible story.

Please, Kind Person

(H)ave the children form their chairs into a circle.

Supplies:
none

Zillies™:
metallic wig

Say: Today's Bible story is about forgiveness—asking for it and giving it to someone else.

Ask: What do you think Jesus would want us to do? (*forgive one another*)

ZONE IN: Jesus teaches us to forgive one another.

Say: We are going to play a game where one person is looking for forgiveness. But the rest of the persons in the group do not want to forgive him or her. However, if a person does give in and forgive IT, then IT and that person will change places.

Explain to the children that IT will come up to each member of the group and ask: "Please, kind person, will you forgive me?" Because no one in the group wants to forgive IT, then each person will respond: "I'm sorry but I can't forgive you." But the person being asked must replay with a straight face. If that person smiles, that means he or she has forgiven IT. Then IT and that player must change places. The only rule is that IT may not touch any of the other players in any way. But IT can make silly faces or use a silly voice in order to plead his or her case. Play until everyone has had a chance to be IT or until the children get bored.

The Unforgiving Servant

by Sharilyn S. Adair

You will need seven characters to act out this story: Narrator, Peter, Jesus, the King, Servant 1, Servant 2, Servant 3, Servant 4, and Narrator. Peter, and Jesus can be played by the children. Or, you may create story puppets by coloring them differently than the other puppets. The remaining characters will be from the story puppets(*Reproducibles 10A and 10B.*) Stretch a towel or a blanket between two chairs. Let the children who are using the story puppets kneel behind this screen and hold their puppets above it. (*Note: The teacher may be the narrator for the story.*)

Narrator: One day after Jesus and his friends had been talking about forgiveness, Peter had a question.

Peter: Jesus, if someone does something wrong to me, how many times should I forgive them? Should I forgive them three times or seven times?

Narrator: Now Peter must have felt that he was being very generous. After all, the law said that three times was enough. But that is not what Jesus answered.

Jesus: Not seven times, but seventy seven times. And the reason you should do this is because God's kingdom is like that.

Narrator: And so Jesus told a story to help Peter understand.
Jesus: A certain king wished to settle accounts with his servants.

King: Aha! One of my servants owes me ten thousand talents. That's more money than he can possibly pay back in his lifetime. Something must be done. I must see this man immediately.

Servant 1: (*Comes before the king.*) You sent for me, your Majesty?

King: Yes. I was going over my accounts and discovered that you owe me a lot of money. I want my money now. Can you pay?

Servant 1: No, your Majesty. But don't worry. I will pay you all that I owe. (*Servant begins to quiver and shake.*)

King: Then I am going to sell you, your wife, your children, and all your possessions in order to get my money back.

Servant 1: Oh, please, please, your Majesty, give me more time to get the money. Honest. I will pay you back all that I owe.

King: You can't possibly raise that much money. But I can tell that you are truly sorry. So I will forgive your debt. As of this moment, you owe me nothing.(*The King leaves the stage.*)

Servant 1: Whew! That was close.

Jesus: And the servant jumped for joy at his good fortune. As he was leaving the palace, however, he came upon a fellow servant. This servant owed him a small amount of money.

Servant 2: (*Enters whistling.*)

Servant 1: You there! What do you think I am, a money bag? Have you forgotten that you owe me money? I want you to pay me now!

Servant 2: Who, me?

Servant 1: Don't try to get away. You know you owe me money.

Servant 2: (*shaking and quivering*) Please, sir, don't shake me so hard. I do not have the money just now. But I will pay later. I promise.

Servant 1: I want the money now! Since you can't pay, I'll have you thrown into prison.

Servant 2: Please have mercy on me. I will pay you. (*Servant 1 drags Servant 2 off the stage. Servant 3 enters and watches.*)

Jesus: When one of the other servants heard what the first servant had done to the second servant, he was most upset.

Servant 3: (*to the king*) Oh, your Majesty, I have seen something terribly unjust. Do you remember the servant whose debt you forgave? One of his friends owed him money. Rather than return the favor and forgive that debt, he had the other servant thrown into prison.

King: Why that ungrateful little wretch. Bring him to me. (*Servant 3 exits and re-enters with servant 1.*)You wicked servant! I forgave your debt because you asked me to. I felt sorry for you. Shouldn't you have done the same for your fellow servant? Because you are so unforgiving, I have changed my mind. You will go to prison until you can pay every cent you owe me.

Narrator: By telling this story, Jesus taught that God is willing to forgive us as we are willing to forgive one another. The end.

Choose one or more activities to immerse your children in the Bible story.

Break the Circle

Push the chairs and tables back in order to create an open space to play this game. It is active and requires space for movement. Have the children join hands and form a circle in the open space. This is a game similar to one played in Ghana called Kholo Eveawo (Two Friends.)

Select one child to be IT. IT comes to the center of the circle.

Say: In today's Bible story Jesus taught us that if we want to be forgiven for our wrongdoings, then we must also forgive others. So what we have are two partners: "I'm sorry" and "You're forgiven." We ask forgiveness when we do wrong. We give forgiveness when someone does wrong to us. Let's play a game to help us remember.

From the center of the circle, IT chooses a pair of children to be the runners. They are identified by IT taking her or his hand and breaking the circle where they are holding hands. The player on the right begins to run counterclockwise around the circle. The player on the left begins to run clockwise around the outside of the circle. When the two children meet about half-way around the circle, one will say "I'm sorry" and the other will respond "You're forgiven." Then both will continue back to the space that is empty. Whoever returns to the space first gets to keep it. The player who comes in second replaces IT in the center of the circle. IT will then assume that space in the circle.

ZONE IN **Jesus teaches us to forgive one another.**

Choose one or more activities to bring the Bible to life.

Sing and Celebrate

(M)ake a copy of the words for each child or create a song chart for the class. Children can also use the kazoos for the first, second, and fourth stanzas.

Supplies:
cassette player

Zillies™:
Cassette, kazoos

God's Gotta Lotta Love

God's gotta lotta love to go around,
go around, go around.
God's gotta lotta love to go around, so
sing a happy sound.
(sing) la la la la la la la la

Gotta lotta love to go around,
go around, go around.
God's gotta lotta love to go around, so
hum a happy sound.
(hum or use kazoos) hm hm hm hm hm hm hm hm

Gotta lotta love to go around,
go around, go around.
God's gotta lotta love to go around, so
whistle a happy sound.
(whistle or use kazoos) la la la la la la la la

Gotta lotta love to go around,
go around, go around.
God's gotta lotta love to go around, so
play a happy sound.
(play kazoos) la la la la la la la la

Gotta lotta love to go around,
go around, go around.
God's gotta lotta love to go around, so
shout a happy sound.
(shout) hip, hip, hooray, hip, hip, hooray.

Gotta lotta love to go around,
go around, go around.
God's gotta lotta love to go around, so
sing a happy sound.

Life Zone ™

Choose one or more activities to bring the Bible to life.

Supplies:
none

Zillies™:
comet ball

Think Fast

Have the children sit on the floor in a circle.

Say: **Whenever we do wrong, Jesus teaches us that we should ask for forgiveness from others. Whenever someone asks forgiveness of us, then Jesus teaches us that we should forgive. Let's see how fast you can do this. I will start with one of the phrases and pitch the comet ball. Whoever catches the ball must then respond with the partner phrase. For example, if I say "I'm sorry" then the person who catches the ball will respond with "You're forgiven."**
Then that person will say "I'm sorry" and throw the ball to another person who will respond with "You're forgiven." Let's see if we can keep the ball going quickly without a mistake.

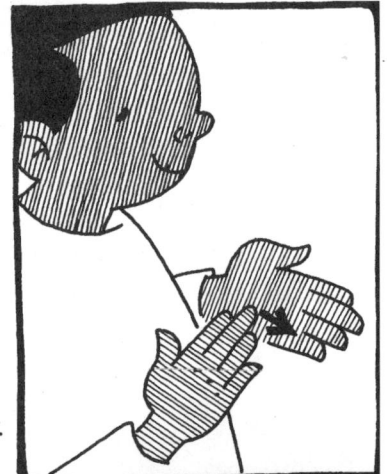

Supplies:
none

Zillies™:
none

Happy Hands

Teach the children the American Sign Language for the Bible verse for today.

Say: **God forgives us when we do wrong. God wants us to forgive one another. Jesus teaches us that if we expected to be forgiven then we had to be ready to forgive too.**

Practice the hand signs. Then read each one of these statements and let the children respond with the Bible verse.

Say: **When someone calls me names** (*pause for response*). **When someone hurts me** (*pause for response*). **When someone makes me feel bad about myself** (*pause for response*). **When I don't do as I'm told** (*pause for response*). **When I mistreat someone** (*pause for response*)**, help me to remember to forgive. Amen.**

Make a copy of HomeZone™ for each family in your class.

forgive one another

126

BibleZone™

Bible Verse
Forgive one another.
Ephesians 4:32, Good News Bible

Bible Story
Matthew 18:21–35

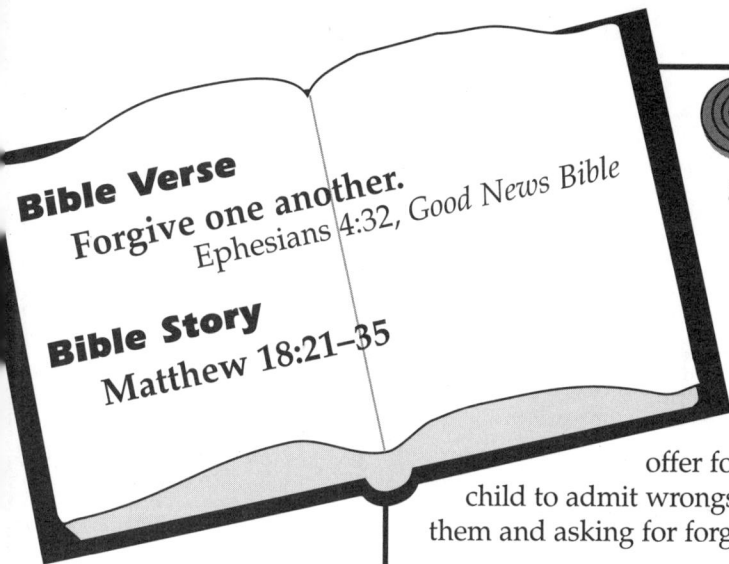

In today's Bible story your child heard about forgiveness. In order for Jesus to get his point across about forgiving one another, he told a story about a servant who had received forgiveness of all of his debts (which were considerable) and yet this servant did not offer this same forgiveness to a fellow debtor. Jesus was pointing out to the disciples that if they wanted to be forgiven, then they had to offer forgiveness to one another. Encourage your child to admit wrongs and to accept responsibility for righting them and asking for forgiveness.

Learning to Say "I'm Sorry"

Learning to say "I'm sorry" is often as difficult for children as it is for adults. Admitting a wrong is a blow to self-esteem. But all persons commit acts that need forgiveness. The hardest part is remembering that we are to make an effort not to commit that act again as a true sign of contrition.

Teach your child the American Sign Language for "I'm sorry." It is done by folding down the fingers of the right hand into a fist with the thumb up. Rub the fist in a small circle on the chest while looking down and contrite.

Using sign language is a good way to reinforce the biblical message. Here is the Bible verse in American Sign Language.

Forgive one another

ZONE IN

Jesus teaches us to forgive one another.

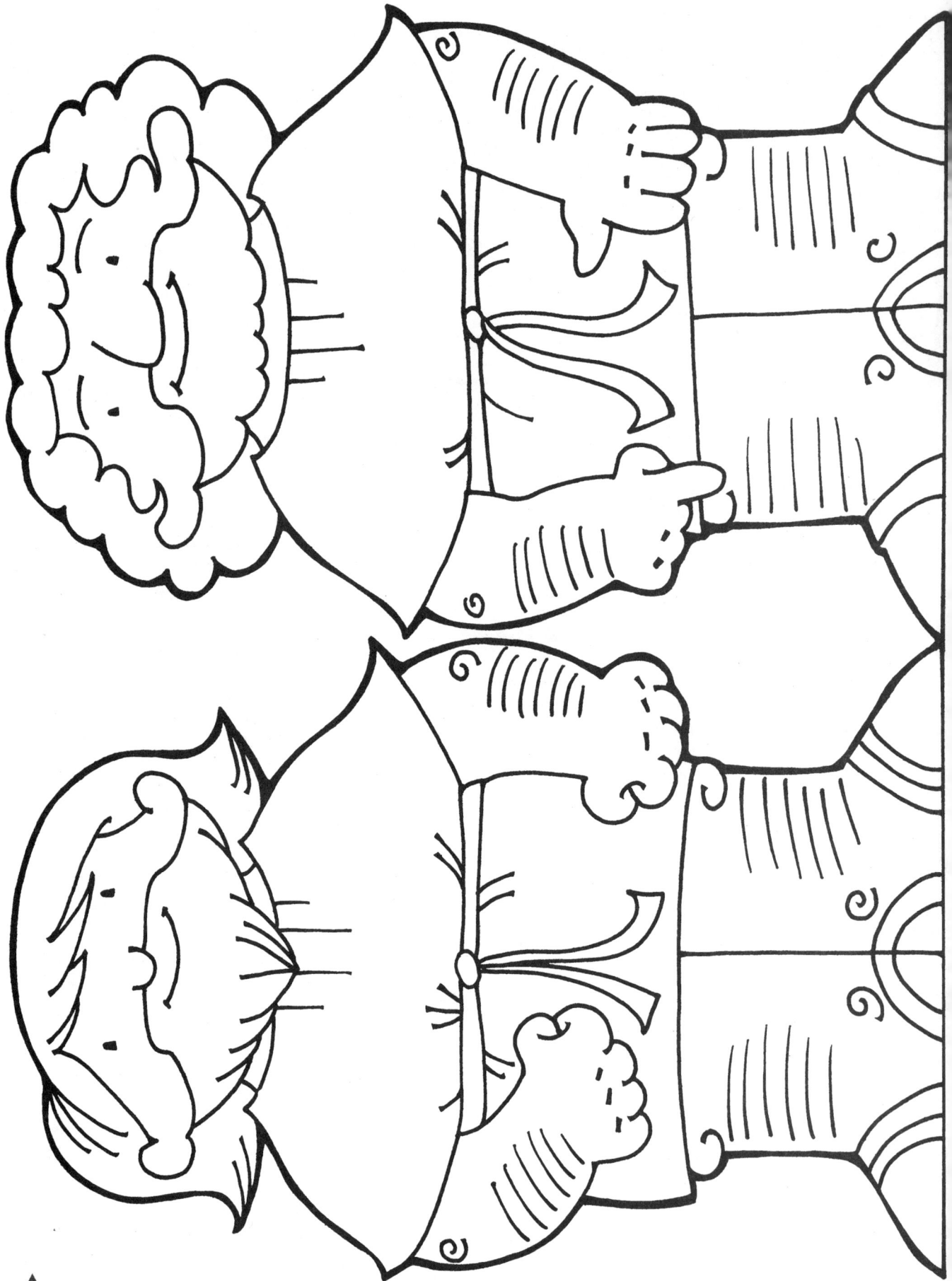

Reproducible 10A

Permission granted to photocopy for local church use. © 1998 Abingdon Press.

BIBLEZONE™

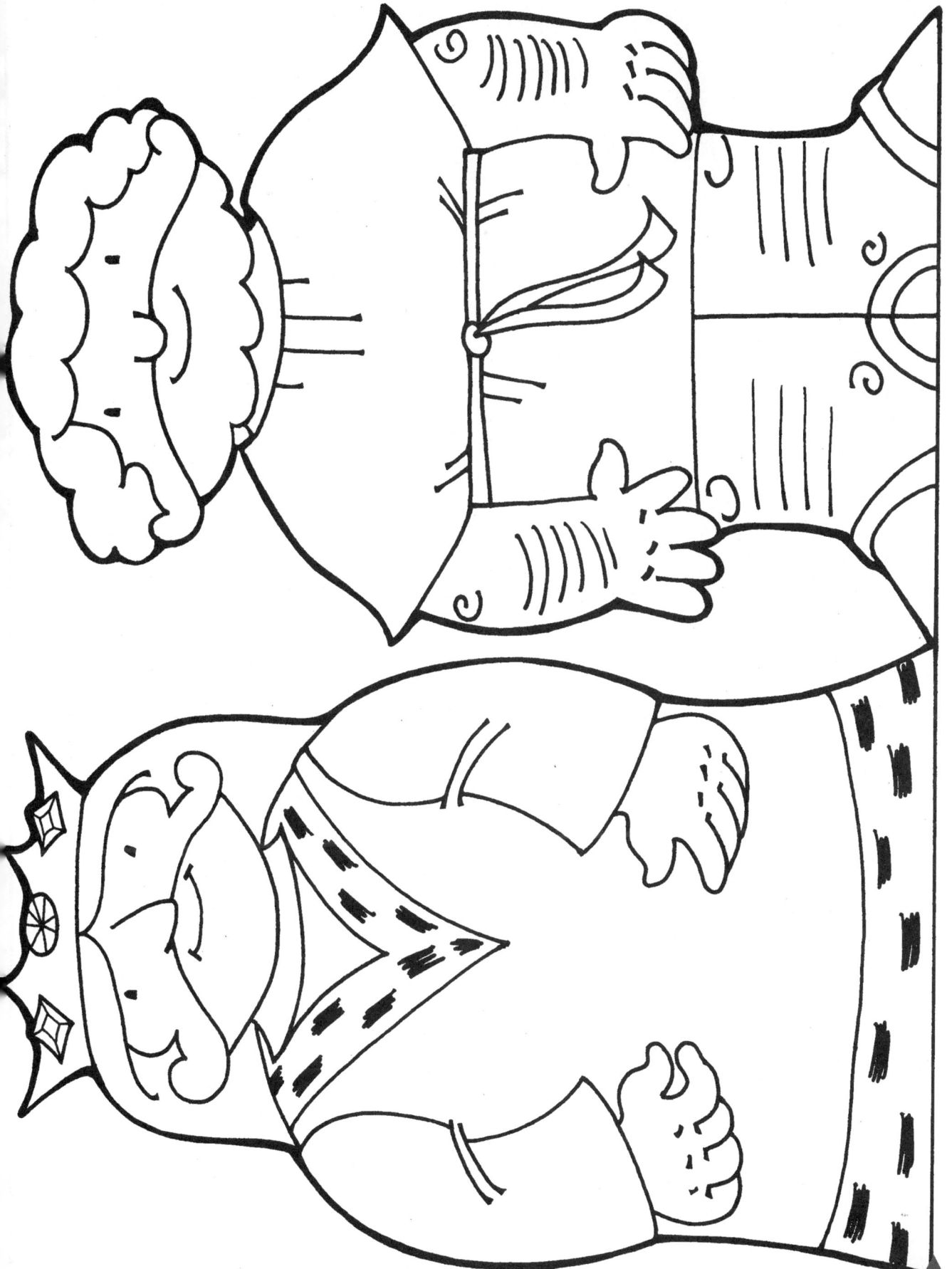

Reproducible 10B

Permission granted to photocopy for local church use. © 1998 Abingdon Press.

Least of These

Enter the Zone™

Bible Verse
Let us love, not in word or speech, but in truth and action.
                    1 John 3:18

Bible Story
Matthew 25:31–45

The parable for today's lesson is often referred to as the parable of the last judgment. This story captures the spirit of what it means to be a follower of Christ. In this final judgment, all the nations are judged, not just Israel. They are separated into the sheep and the goats. The sheep are those worthy to enter the kingdom; the goats are those who are not. The decision is made based on acts of mercy performed for the less fortunate. It is not how righteous a person appears to be, but how a person lives out the faith that is important. A surprising element is that those who are welcomed into the kingdom have no consciousness of their actions.

According to Jesus, God expects us to minister to the needs of others. When we love God, ministering to others is a response to that love. God wants action,not words.

The concrete images of this parable were not lost on Jesus' audience. In Bible lands, herds of sheep and goats would have been separated by the shepherd. The right hand was also the side of honor and blessing. Jesus was subtly letting the people know that God was not fooled by false appear-

ances and would have no trouble in recognizing who was a true child of God.

Most younger elementary children are easily touched by the needs of others and are even willing to give up their most treasured possession if someone else needs it. Their generous spirit is the spirit of giving that Jesus was talking about. Only as they become adults do they begin to put a price tag on the fruits of their generosity.

Children have a unique ability to discover ways to be of service. They are quite capable of offering kindness and performing acts within the church and community. Encourage them to identify those in need around them and to plan ways to serve. Remind the children that when they love God, their love for God automatically shows up in the love for others.

Jesus teaches us to serve God by serving one another.

Scope the ZONE ™

ZONE	TIME	SUPPLIES	⊚ ZILLIES™
Zoom Into the Zone			
Make Racing Turtles	10 minutes	Reproducible 11A, six-inch paper plates, tape, glue, or stapler and staples, crayons or felt-tip markers, scissors	none
Turtle Races	10 minutes	Racing Turtles, long tables or linoleum floor, masking tape	none
BibleZone™			
Twitch, Shake, Wiggle	5 minutes	none	none
The Sheep and the Goats	10 minutes'	Reproducible 11A, scissors	none
Sheep and Goats	5 minutes	Reproducible 11A (sheep and goat cards), blindfold	none
LifeZone			
Sing and Celebrate	5 minutes	cassette player	Cassette
Ready for Action!	10 minutes	Reproducible 11B, scissors, masking tape	none
Prayer in Motion	5 minutes	none	none

⊚ Zillies™ are found in the **BibleZone™ FUNspirational™ Kit.**

Choose one or more activities to catch your children's interest.

Supplies:
Reproducible 11A, tape, glue, or stapler and staples, crayons or felt-tip markers, six-inch paper plates, scissors

Zillies™:
none

Make Racing Turtles

Make a copy of the turtle parts (*Reproducible 11A*) for each child in the group. Cut the turtle parts from the sheep and goats. Save those until a later activity.

Greet the children as they arrive. Let them begin working on their racing turtles. Show them how to decorate their turtle shells (six-inch paper plates) and then assemble the turtles. Make a slit from one edge to the center of the plate. Overlap slightly and staple on the edge to create a slight cone shape. Then attach the turtle head, legs, and tail.

Ask: **When you see a turtle what do you think of?** (*slow*)

Say: **But we are making racing turtles. Our turtles are going to be the opposite of what you think of when you think of a turtle.**

Turtle Races

When all the children have completed their racing turtles, let them draw numbers from the basket. This will determine their racing order. Let the children line up according to their numbers. Place the work tables together side by side (if the tables in your class are long.) You will need about a six-foot raceway. If you do not have long tables and have a linoleum floor, mark off a six-foot track on that surface.

Say: **When you think about turtles, you think about slow. A turtle has never been known for its speed on the land.**

Ask: **Who would win a race between a turtle and a rabbit? between a turtle and a cheetah? between a turtle and a jet plane?**

Say: **In today's Bible story we learn that it is not always the one you expect who will be the most important.**

Let the first four children race against each other by blowing on their turtles. Continue in small groups until all children have raced. Then pit the winners against one another.

cut to center of paper plate

staple

tape to underside

tape to underside

Bible Zone™

Choose one or more activities to immerse your children in the Bible story.

Twitch, Shake, Wiggle

Supplies:
none

Zillies™:
none

Say: Today's Bible verse says that we are to love, not in word or speech, but in truth and action. Let's play a game where we do not use a word, but use an action instead.

Bring everyone together in a circle. The first player begins by saying, "The baby went to sleep." The rest of the group answers, "How did the baby go to sleep?" The first player then says, "The baby went to sleep like this, like this," repeating a small gesture such as nodding the head or twisting the wrist. The rest of the group mimics the gesture and answers, "Like this, like this."

The entire group continues to repeat the gesture as the next player in line says, "The baby went to sleep," and the others respond as before. The second player adds another gesture to the first, so that now there are two movements to keep going. The game continues around the circle, each player adding a gesture. By the end of the game, the entire group should be twitching, shaking, wiggling and shaking all over the place.

Ask the children: What do you think it means that God wants us to love in truth and action, not word and speech? (*It's more important to do something than to talk about doing something and not do it.*)

Say: I am going to give you a setting and what happened. You decide whether it is words (Yakkety Yak) or actions (Zoom.)

1. "I promise to do my homework first," said Zack. But Zack watched television instead. (Yakkety Yak)
2. "I won't ride my bicycle in the street anymore," said Jill. Jill kept her bike on the sidewalk until she was a better rider. (Zoom)
3. "I'll put a quarter of my allowance each week in the mission offering," said Alexander. But on Sunday he had already spent his allowance. (Yakkety Yak)
4. "I'll help clean the garage on Saturday," promised Megan. But she forgot that her soccer team was having a picnic in the park. (Yakkety Yak)
5. "I'll read you a story after supper," said Willie. After helping his mother clear the table, Willie read his little brother a story. (Zoom)

Zone In: **Jesus teaches us to serve God by serving one another.**

The Sheep and the Goats

Say: Today's story is about sheep and goats, but it's really a story about people. I am going to pass around a basket of pictures. Each of you will take one. You will either be a sheep or a goat (*Reproducible 11A.*)

Have the children form two groups. All the sheep will be in one group. All the goats will be in the other group.

Say: We're going to hear the Bible story in a special way today. The Sheep and the Goats are two different kinds of people. Sheep, you are people who are kind. When I come to you needing help, you will decide what you can do for me, no matter what it takes. Goats, when I come to your group, you are to refuse to do anything that would help me out. No matter what I ask for, think of some reason why you can't help me. You can use excuses such as that you are too busy or that you might get dirty.

Ask: Does everyone understand what to do?

Story 1:
I was traveling through your town when my car broke down. It is late, and all the auto repair places are closed. Not only that, but I don't have my billfold and checkbook. I accidentally left them at the restaurant where I ate dinner one hundred miles back. I called the restaurant, and thank goodness they have my billfold and checkbook. They will hold them for me until I can get back there. I don't know what to do about tonight, though. I can't get the car fixed until morning, and I have no money or credit cards with me to pay for a room in a hotel or motel. Can you help?

Story 2:
I go to your school. The weather has been cold this week, and I do not have a sweater or coat. Our family is poor. We don't have money to buy clothes right now. What will you do?

Story 3:
I am an elderly person living alone in your neighborhood. I have a bad case of the flu, and the doctor says that I need to stay in bed and rest. I feel weak whenever I try to get up, anyway. I have a little dog who gets lonesome and needs to be walked. Can you help me?

Story 4:

I am in a state prison near your town. My relatives are ashamed of me and will not come to visit me, so I have no contact with anyone outside this prison. When the prison has visiting hours, I just stay in my cell and read. I wish somebody cared about me enough to visit me. Can you help me?

Each of these stories are events that might actually happen to one of us today. But these stories help us to think about what Jesus wants us to do. Jesus' friends also wanted to know how to be good people and so Jesus told them a story:

Pretend you are like a flock of sheep. The end of the day comes. I will gather all the flock in front of me and I will separate them into two groups. I will put the sheep at my right hand. (*Have all the sheep move to the right side of the teacher.*) I will put all the goats at my left hand. (*Have the goats move to the left side.*) To the sheep I will say, "You are welcome to come into my sheepfold, for you have been kind and generous. When I was hungry, you gave me food. When I was thirsty, you gave me something to drink. When I was a stranger, you welcomed me. When I was without clothing, you gave me something to wear. When I was sick, you took care of me. When I was in prison, you visited me.

The sheep will be very confused.

They will ask, "When did we see you hungry and give you food, or thirsty and give you something to drink? When were you a stranger that we welcomed you or without clothing that we gave you something to wear? When were you sick or in prison that we visited you?

The shepherd would answer them, "Whenever you do it to one of my children, it is as though you had done it to me."

Then the shepherd will turn to the goats and say, "Go away from me. For I was hungry, and you gave me no food. I was thirsty, and you gave me nothing to drink. I was a stranger, and you did not welcome me. I was without clothing, and you did not give me anything to wear. I was sick, and in prison, and yet you stayed away."

And the goats will be very, very confused and ask the shepherd, "When did we see you hungry or thirsty, or without clothing, or sick, or in prison, and do nothing to help you?

And the shepherd will answer them, "What you did not do for one of my children, you did not do to me."

Through this story the people learned that to serve God they were to serve one another.

Choose one or more activities to immerse your children in the Bible story.

Supplies:
Reproducible 11A, blindfold

Zillies™:
none

Sheep and Goats

Say: **When Jesus told a story to the people using sheep and goats as examples, the people would know just what he was talking about. Being a shepherd was an occupation that most people in Palestine knew about. Shepherds often separated the sheep from the goats. It was very easy to do. Usually the goats were even a different color. Jesus was saying that appearances didn't matter. It would be easy to tell the difference between those who lived a faithful life and served others and those who didn't. Let's play a game and see if our shepherd can find all of her or his sheep among the goats.**

Select one child to be the shepherd (*Reproducible 11A*). Blindfold that player. Collect the sheep and goat cards and shuffle them. Let the children redraw. Once each child has determined whether he or she is a sheep or a goat, let the children scatter about the open area of the room. Pay close attention that the blindfolded shepherd does not wander into areas where injury might occur.

Say: **In this game the only sound you can make is that of sheep (*imitate the sound*) and that of a goat (*imitate that sound*.) Whenever the shepherd calls out "Where are you, sheep?" then everyone must make the sound of either the sheep or the goats. If the shepherd finds a sheep, then the sheep must follow right behind the shepherd as the search continues.**

Play the game until the shepherd has discovered all the sheep. Then let the last sheep found, be the shepherd in the next game.

ZONE IN™ | **Jesus teaches us to serve God by serving one another.**

Life ZONE™

Choose one or more activities to bring the Bible to life.

Sing and Celebrate

Supplies;
cassette player

Zillies™;
Cassette

(M)ake a copy of the words for each child or create a class songchart. Divide the group into three sections: Freezing Woman, Thirsty Man, and Group. Sing the song together.

The Blessing
Freezing Woman
Bless you, my child, for you have been a blessing.
May the good Lord smile down upon you this day,
for you gave me kindness when I was in need.
God bless you, my child, as you have blessed me.

Group
Bless you, my child, for you have been a blessing.
May the good Lord smile down upon you this day,
for you gave her kindness when she was in need.
(Woman) God bless you, my child, as you have blessed me.

Thirsty Man:
Bless you, my child, for you have been a blessing.
May the good Lord smile down upon you this day,
for you gave me kindness when I was in need.
God bless you, my child, as you have blessed me.

Woman and Man:
You shared a part of you, the heart of who you are.
You did not know me, yet you showed me love.

Group
Bless you, my child, for you have been a blessing.
May the good Lord smile down upon you this day,
for you gave them kindness when they were in need.

Thirsty Man:
God bless you, my child, as you have blessed me.

Life Zone™

Choose one or more activities to bring the Bible to life.

Supplies:
Reproducible 11B, scissors, masking tape

Zillies™:
none

Ready for Action!

Make a copy of the action items *(Reproducible 11B)* so that each child has one object. Cut the squares apart. Tape the squares on the floor and have the children find a square to stand on.

Say: Jesus teaches us that we are to show love to God by showing love to others. Each of you is standing on an object that represents a way to serve God by serving others. Identify your object and as a group we will decide how that can be a help to someone else. *(The clock connotes time that a person spends with someone else.)*

Give the children time to discuss how each item might be needed by someone.

Then say: Let's play a game. This game resembles a game that children in Sweden play called "The Number Game." But instead of standing on numbers we will be standing on service items.

Select one child to be IT. IT will call out two items. The players with those two items must change places. IT tries to get to one of the items first. If IT fails, then IT must call out two other items. If IT succeeds, the player left without an item becomes IT for the next item.

Supplies:
none

Zillies™:
none

Prayer in Motion

Say: Prayers don't always have to be quiet and still. Sometimes prayers can be very active. After all Jesus told his friends that God wanted action not just words. So let's put our prayer into action. Everyone stand up where you are. Give yourself plenty of room.

(Jump up with hands outstretched.) **Say: Thank you, God, for everything!** *(Bend down and touch the floor.)* **Thank you, God, for the earth and all that is on it.** *(Turn around..)* **Thank you, God, for all the people everywhere.** *(Lean to one side.)* **Thank you, God, for food.** *(Lean to the other side.)* **Thank you, God, for clothing.** *(Hug self.)* **Thank you, God, for friends.** *(Leap and dance.)* **Help me to be a joyful servant. Amen.**

Make a copy of HomeZone for each family in your class.

Bible Verse

Let us love, not in word or speech, but in truth and action.

1 John 3:18

Bible Story

Matthew 25:31–45

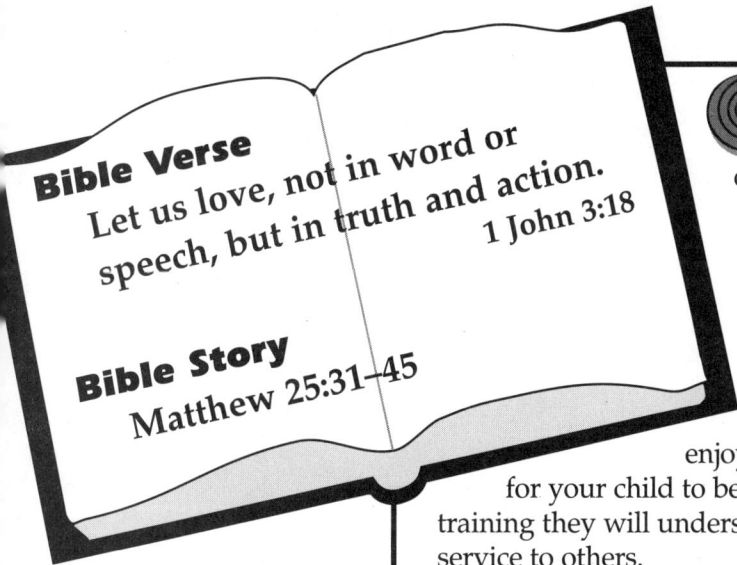

In today's Bible lesson, your child heard the story sometimes called the parable of the last judgment. In this story that Jesus told, Jesus compared people to sheep and goats. The sheep were the ones who lived faithful lives of kindness and service. The goats were the ones that did not reach out to others. Your child is at a point in his or her life where service to others is not a job but a pleasure. Children at this age enjoy doing things for others. Find opportunities for your child to be a part of a service project. Through this training they will understand what it means to serve God through service to others.

Lenten Calendar

Look on your calendar and discover when Lent begins. Lent is the forty days (not counting Sundays) before Easter. Make a grid that has spaces for forty-seven days. Make sure the spaces are big enough for stickers or small drawings. Mount the grid onto wrapping paper or colorful construction paper.

Lent is a time of self-sacrifice as we remember the gift that Jesus gave to us. Let your child perform acts of service during this time as his or her gift to Jesus. Each time an act of service is performed, let your child add a sticker or a small drawing to that particular day.

Have a special prayer time during Lent. Remember people who are hungry, those who are sick, those who are homeless, and those who are needy. This is a time to help your child look outside of him- or herself.

Jesus teaches us to serve God by serving one another.

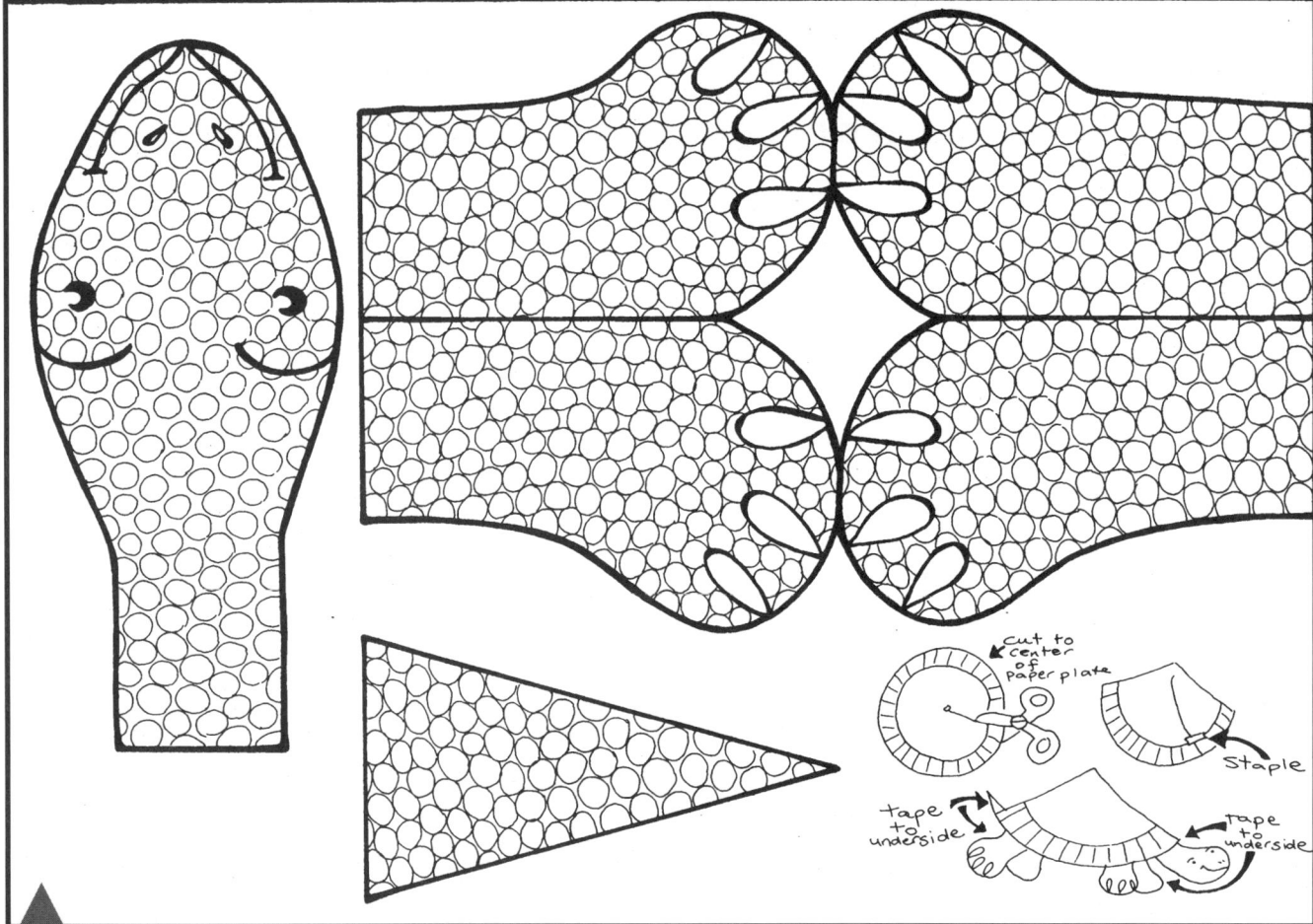

cut to center of paper plate

staple

tape to underside

tape to underside

Reproducible 11A

BIBLEZONE™

Reproducible 11B

Birds of the Field

Enter the Zone™

Bible Verse
Leave all your worries with God, because God cares for you.

1 Peter 5:7, adapted

Bible Story
Matthew 6:25–33

In the Bible story for today, Jesus describes God as the Creator and Sustainer of all life. If God cares for birds and lilies, then certainly God will also care for and provide for God's people.

The people of God, Jesus said, should not worry about food and clothing, because life is more than basic needs. Further, we cannot change our lives by worrying. Jesus was not saying that these needs are unimportant. Neither did he mean that we should not work or be diligent. Anyone who watches birds knows that they are very hard workers.

What Jesus was saying is that our concern should be first on how to fulfill what God wants. Only when we put our trust in God to care for and provide for us do our anxieties about life begin to lessen. Awareness of our dependence on God for sustenance of life frees us to focus on what God wants us to be and to do and to strive to live in obedience to God.

Each younger elementary child is just beginning to expand her or his concept of God. It is important, therefore, that your teaching about God centers on the understanding that God is Creator, God is provider, God is dependable, and God is love. We certainly hope that none of the children we encounter in our classrooms will know anxiety about their basic needs, but the reality is that not all children live in loving and caring environments. Their most basic needs for love and acceptance may not be met. As a teacher of school-age children, you are called to model God's love to all your children. Show them acceptance and understanding. In order to trust God, they must first be able to experience trust in the individuals around them.

Children's self-esteem is fortified by feeling that they are important to someone. Today's lesson can help them realize how precious they are to God. The things children have, the houses they live in, and the kinds of clothes they wear are not the things that make them important in God's eyes.

Jesus teaches us to trust in God.

Scope the ZONE ™

ZONE	TIME	SUPPLIES	⊙ ZILLIES™
Zoom Into the Zone			
Silly Bear	10 minutes	Reproducible 12A, fabric scraps, scissors, white glue, construction paper, bits of lace, artificial flowers, feathers, faux jewels, spray mount, posterboard	none
Rabbit in the Hole	10 minutes	none	none
BibleZone™			
Something Bad About Something Good	5 minutes	none	none
Consider the Lilies	5 minutes	none	none
Trust Me	10 minutes	plastic hoola hoop, blindfold, string or yarn, large piece of paper, felt-tip pens	laser shooter and disks
LifeZone			
Sing and Celebrate	5 minutes	cassette player	Cassette, kazoos
Awesome Aviary	10 minutes	Reproducible 12B, scissors, crayons or felt-tip markers, stapler, staples, facial or bathroom tissue, glue, yarn, (Option: googly eyes)	none
What, Me Worry?	5 minutes	none	none

⊙ Zillies™ are found in the **BibleZone™ FUNspirational™ Kit.**

Zoom Into the Zone™

Choose one or more activities to catch your children's interest.

Supplies:
Reproducible 12A, fabric scraps, scissors, white glue, construction paper, bits of lace, artificial flowers, feathers, faux jewels, spray mount, posterboard

Zillies™:
none

Silly Bear

Make a copy of Silly Bear (*Reproducible 12A*) for each child in your group. You will also need an assortment of fabric scraps, notions, faux jewels, sequins, construction paper, feathers, and other decorative items for the children to use to create clothing for their bears. If you have the time, mount Silly Bear on posterboard so that he will be steadier to work with.

Greet the children warmly as they come into the room. Direct them to a work space where all the supplies are available.

Say: Each of you has a Silly Bear. Silly Bear is afraid that his natural fur coat just won't do when he starts to school (or use some other event that is familiar to your children.) Silly Bear wants you to help him look his best. I want you to dress Silly Bear. Silly Bear knows you will make him look his best.

As the children finish their project, **ask: Do you think a bear looks silly wearing clothing? Why? Did God provide just the kind of outside covering that a bear needs wherever it lives?**

Say: God cares for all the animals. God cares for us. In today's Bible story Jesus teaches a lesson about not worrying but putting our trust in God.

Supplies:
none

Zillies™:
none

Rabbit in the Hole

Say: God had a plan for all living things. Each living thing is specially suited for the place that it lives. Each living thing is specially suited for the food that it eats and the shelter that it seeks or builds. Let's play a game of shelter. The game is called Rabbit in the Hole. The object of the game is for the rabbit to get away from the fox by seeking shelter in a burrow. But there is only room for one rabbit in each burrow.

Have the children form pairs. One child will stand in front of the other. Let the pairs space themselves around the room. The one in the back is the rabbit. This will change throughout the game. Select one of the pairs of children to be the fox and one to be the rabbit. The fox wants to have rabbit for dinner. The rabbit is trying to escape. If the rabbit comes to one of the burrows (pairs of children), then the rabbit on the back must leave and seek another burrow before it is caught by the fox. If the fox catches the rabbit, then the roles are reversed and the fox becomes the rabbit.

Bible ZONE ™

Choose one or more activities to immerse your children in the Bible story.

Something Bad About Something Good

Supplies:
none

Zillies™:
none

Bring the children together in a circle on the floor.

Say: Most of us are very lucky. We have a place to live and clothing to wear and friends and family who love us. We really don't have much to complain about when you think about some other people in our country or in the world. And yet, we still complain. We act as though we are looking for the bad things in all the good things we have. Let's play a game and see if we can think of bad qualities of some very nice things. I want each of you to think of an object that you like very much. It can be a favorite toy, a favorite place to go, a favorite food, or a favorite pet. (*Give the children time to think of an object.*)

Ask: Have you got the object firmly in your mind?

Say: Now I want you to think of all the bad qualities about that object. For example, if the object I thought about was an ice cream cone, I might think about the fact that it's fattening, you can't eat it on a hot day, or it makes my teeth hurt. Now I want you to describe your object to the group using only the bad things about it. Let's see if we can guess what it is.

Give each child a chance to describe her or his object. Encourage them to make it sound as awful as they can without lying. If everyone is stumped and the player has run out of bad things to say, suggest the player give one "good" clue. The first person to guess what it is gets the next chance to describe something.

Say: It's silly to try to think bad things about very nice things, but sometimes when we complain and complain, that is what we are doing. In today's Bible story Jesus teaches us to quit worrying about this small stuff. After all, God is in charge.

ZONE IN ™

> ### Jesus teaches us to trust God.

Consider the Lilies

by Sharilyn S. Adair

Explain to the children that today they can experience one of of Jesus' teachings, not just with their ears but with their whole bodies. Invite them to follow your movements as you repeat Jesus' words. Begin by standing in a relaxed manner with your hands at your sides. Try to make all of your movements smooth and flowing.

You will need to practice this reading several times in order to coordinate your movements with the words. Memorizing the passage would be helpful. Or tape-record yourself reading the passage, then play the taped version as you silently lead the children in making the movements.

Therefore I tell you
(*Bring one hand up slowly to mouth, palm side down, fingers together, thumb underneath. Move hand away from mouth on the word "tell".*)

Do not worry about your life
(*Frown and touch forehead with both hands, palms down.*)

What you will eat
(*Touch mouth with one hand as though putting food in it.*)

or what you will drink
(*Move hand away from mouth, then cup it into drinking glass and move it back to mouth.*)

or about your body, what you will wear
(*Bring both hands to sides, under shoulders, and move them down to waist.*)

Is not life more than food and the body more than clothing?
(*Touch one hand to mouth as though putting food in it, then repeat previous movement.*)

Look at the birds of the air:
(*Raise both arms from sides out and up in front, and look up.*)

They neither sow nor reap nor gather into barns
(*Hold one hand cupped at side like a bag of seed. Put other had into it, then fling that hand out as though sowing seed. Then reach both arms out in front and bring them in to waist to show gathering.*)

and yet your heavenly Father feeds them.
(*Swing one hand out and down from waist and wiggle fingers as though scattering bird seed.*)

Are you not of more value than they?
(*Bend both arms at elbows and bring hands up to shoulders, palms out.*)

And can any of you by worrying add a single hour to your span of life?
(*Touch forehead with both hands, palms down, and frown.*)

And why do you worry about clothing?
(*Bring both hands to sides, under shoulders, and move them down to waist.*)

Consider the lilies of the field, how they grow
(*Squat on floor, then raise up slowly bringing arms up and out like flowers unfolding.*)

They neither toil nor spin
(*Hold one arm straight out in front and bring other hand close to it as you move that hand in circles.*)

Yet I tell you even Solomon in all his glory was not clothed like one of these.
(*Stand proudly and hold both hands with palms touching side of forehead, fingers pointing up.*)

Therefore do not worry, saying, "What will we eat?" or "What will we drink? or What will we wear?"
(*Touch both hands to forehead for worry, bring one hand to mouth for eat, put same hand down, cup it, then bring it back to mouth for drink, bring both hands to sides, under shoulders, and move them down to waist for wear.*)

Your heavenly Father knows that you need all these things.
(*Bring both arms in front, palms together and toward face, and raise them above head as you look upward.*)

But strive first for the kingdom of God and his righteousness, and all these things will be given to you as well.
(*Extend arms out at shoulders, palms up, and bow head.*)

Bible Zone™

Supplies:

plastic hoola hoop,
blindfold, string
or yarn, large
piece of paper,
felt-tip pens

Zillies™:

laser shooter and
disks

Trust Me

Attach a piece of string from the ceiling of the room. If you have heavy-duty rug yarn, you may use that. Attach the string to the rim of a large plastic hoola hoop. (If a hoola hoop is not available, any kind of target will do. Make sure it is large enough not to make the game impossible. Make sure there is nothing behind the target that can be easily knocked over and broken.

Divide the children into pairs and have the pairs stand together in a line.

Say: In today's Bible story Jesus told people to trust God to take care of them. Trusting is not always easy. We always want to do it ourselves. Let's see how well you can trust your friends. Each pair will have a chance to earn points. One will be the shooter. The other will be the sighter. The shooter will be blindfolded. The sighter will tell the shooter how to aim. If the shooter gets one of the laser disks to go through the hoop, that team collects ten points. Each team will have four disks and two turns.

Show the children how to load the laser shooter with a flying disk. After the shooter of each team has had a turn, then the sighters become shooters and go around a second time. Collect points. The sighter can stand behind the shooter or beside the shooter. The only requirement is that the sighter cannot touch the shooter in any way. All instructions must be verbal.

After everyone has had a chance to sight and shoot, **ask: Was it difficult to trust your partner when you couldn't see what you were doing?**

Say: Jesus asks us to trust God to provide for us. The most important thing we can do is try to live as God wants us to live. If we do that, then God will provide the rest.

Jesus teaches us to trust God.

Sing and Celebrate

Supplies:
cassette player

Zillies™:
Cassette, kazoos

Make a copy of the words for each child or create a song chart for the class. Children can also use the kazoos for the first, second, and fourth stanzas.

God's Gotta Lotta Love

God's gotta lotta love to go around,
go around, go around.
God's gotta lotta love to go around, so
sing a happy sound.
La la la la la la la la

God's gotta lotta love to go around,
go around, go around.
God's gotta lotta love to go around, so
hum a happy sound.
Hm hm hm hm hm hm hm hm

God's gotta lotta love to go around,
go around, go around.
God's gotta lotta love to go around, so
whistle a happy sound.
(whistle)

God's gotta lotta love to go around,
go around, go around.
God's gotta lotta love to go around, so
play a happy sound.
(play bottles or kazoos)

God's gotta lotta love to go around,
go around, go around.
God's gotta lotta love to go around, so
shout a happy sound.
(shout) hip, hip, hooray, hip, hip, hooray.

God's gotta lotta love to go around,
go around, go around.
God's gotta lotta love to go around, so
sing a happy sound.

Life zone

Supplies:
Reproducible 12B, scissors, crayons or felt-tip markers, stapler, staples, facial or bathroom tissue, glue, yarn, (Option: googly eyes

Zillies™:
none

Awesome Aviary

Make a copy of the stuffed bird (*Reproducible 12B*) for each child in the group.

Say: In today's Bible story Jesus taught us to trust God. If God provides for the birds and the flowers, then certainly God cares for us. Instead of worrying about all sorts of things, we should just try to live as God taught us and God will provide what we need. Let's make birds to hang in our room—bright, colorful birds—that will remind us to quit worrying and put our trust in God.

Have the children decorate their birds prior to cutting them out. Remind them that if they want their birds to look alike on both sides, they may copy the same design. Cut out and assemble the bird bodies first. Staple around the outside edges, leaving the top parts open so that the children may stuff the birds lightly with facial or bathroom tissue. Then finish stapling. Do the wings the same way. Glue both wings on the bird body. Then attach yarn and hang the birds from the ceiling of the class.

Say: These birds will remind us to leave our worries with God because God cares for us.

Supplies:
none

Zillies™:
none

What, Me Worry?

Bring the children together in the storytelling or worship area.

Say: Everybody worries about something sometime. Let's go around the circle and each of us will share something that we worry about. After each person, the group will say, "Don't worry. God cares for you." I'll start. (*Contribute some worry that you have and let the group respond.*)

When everyone has made a contribution, have the children join hands as they are seated.

Pray: Dear God, help us to trust you to take care of us. Help us to put our worries in your hands because we know you care for us. Amen.

Make a copy of HomeZone for each family in your class.

Bible Verse
Leave all your worries with God, because God cares for you.
1 Peter 5:7, adapted

Bible Story
Matthew 6:25–33

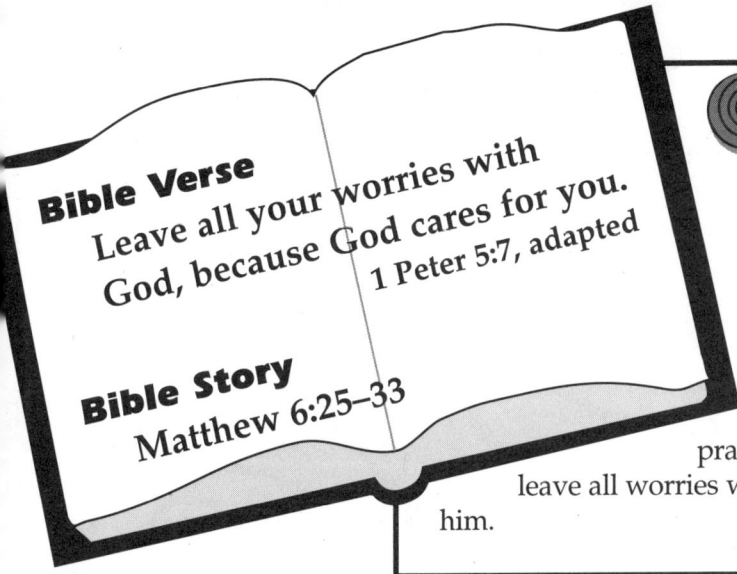

In today's Scripture lesson your child heard Jesus teach his followers to trust God. God cares for the birds of the air and the lilies of the field. Certainly, people are more valuable to God than the birds. So if God cares for them, then God will care for us as well. Children often have secret worries that adults never know about. Encourage your child to share worries. Include those worries in the child's bedtime prayers. Remind your child that he or she can leave all worries with God, and that God cares about her or him.

A Collection of Things

Most of us have a large collection of Things. Things are those items that to many people in other parts of the world would be luxuries. But we simply think of them as important Things. We worry about our Things being stolen. We worry that other people have more Things than we do. Sometimes we worry more about our things than we do the people in our lives.

Think about the people who have fewer Things than you. Make a special tour of your home as a family. Make a special mission offering for all the Things you have.

1. For every television set in your house, put in 25 cents.
2. For every VCR in your house, put in 25 cents.
3. For every CD player or stereo or portable radio, put in 25 cents.
4. For every car in your family, put in 10 cents per car.
5. If you have a personal computer, put in 25 cents. If you have more than one computer, put in 25 cents for each computer.
6. For every telephone in your house, put in 10 cents.
7. If you have as many bathrooms as you have people, put in 10 cents for each bathroom.
8. For every room in your house, put in 10 cents.

Zone In

Jesus teaches us to trust God.

Reproducible 12A

BibleZone™

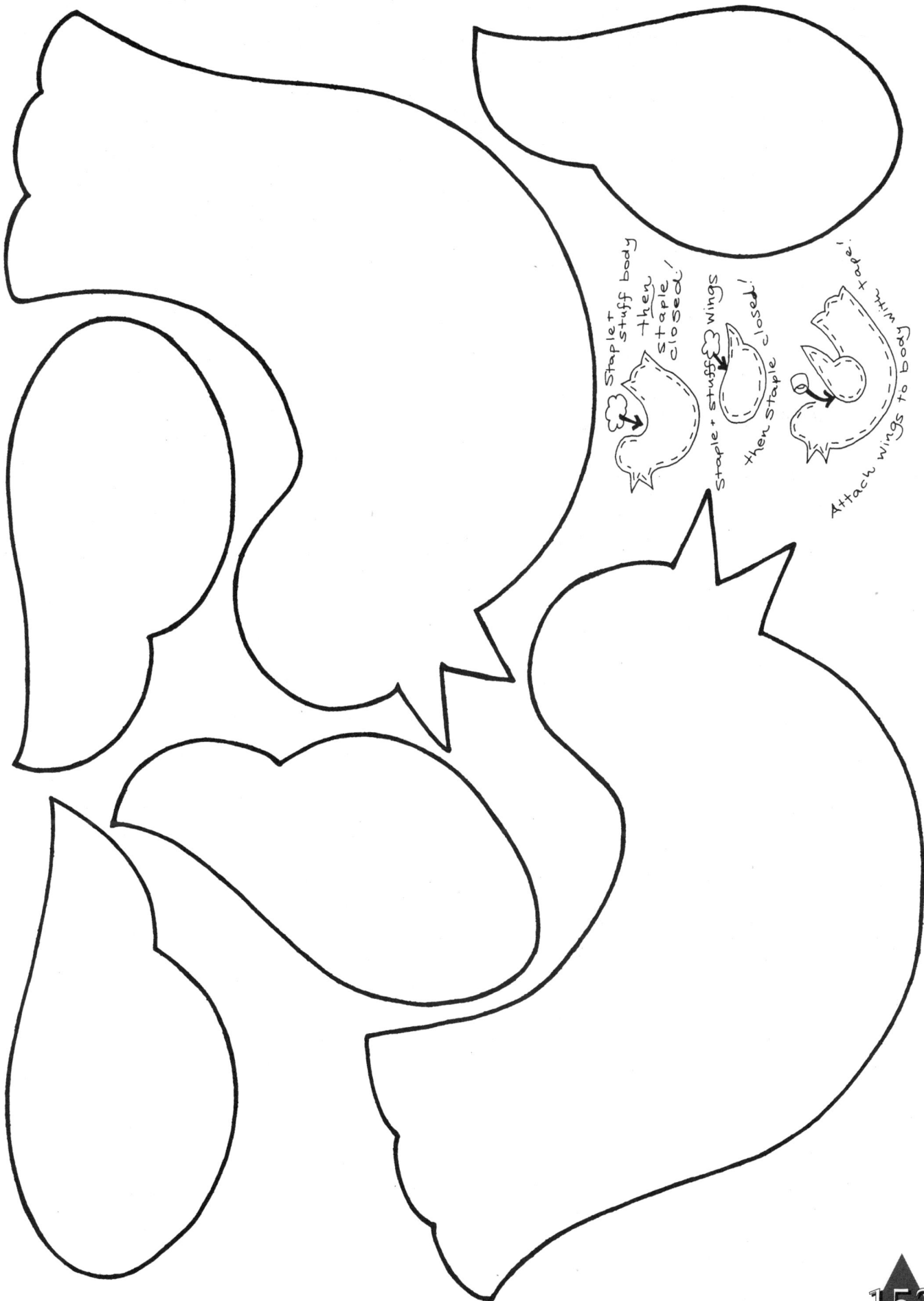

Staple +
stuff body
then
staple
closed!

Staple + stuff wings
then staple closed.

Attach wings to body with tape.

Reproducible 12B

Permission granted to photocopy for local church use. © 1998 Abingdon Press.

The Golden Rule

Enter the ZONE™

Bible Verse
Do to others as you would have them do to you.
Matthew 7:12

Bible Story
Matthew 7:12

What we know as the Golden Rule is found in one form or another not only in Judaism but also in several other religious traditions. In the traditions of Jesus' day, however, the Golden Rule was presented in a negative form: people were called to avoid doing to others what they would not like to have done to themselves. Jesus reinvented it for his followers as a summation of the commandment to love one's enemies. Jesus' challenge to us is to go beyond simply not doing wrong. As Christians, we are called to go the extra mile. The Golden Rule says to us that we should think about others and their happiness.

The Golden Rule summarizes the instructions that Jesus gives for holy living. The author of Matthew explains why the Golden Rule was included, stating that it explains the law of Moses and the prophets.

Matthew's gospel seeks to connect Jesus' teaching to Jewish tradition. Jesus has restated the law, and that is why it is important to us as Christians. Without the

context of holy living in which Jesus places the Golden Rule, it could be used to justify inappropriate behavior rooted in sinful human desire. This is clearly not Jesus' message. Instead, he was teaching mutual respect and compassion, summarizing his teachings on right living under the law.

Younger elementary children are beginning to empathize with others. They are able to put themselves into the places of others at least to some extent. They do know how they want to be treated, and probably know, from experience, that wrong behavior often illicits bad responses in those they are playing with. But the Golden Rule is more than this. It means not only not to do bad things, but to do good things even though the person on the receiving end may not reciprocate.

Jesus teaches us to treat others as we want to be treated.

Scope the ZONE

ZONE	TIME	SUPPLIES	⊚ ZILLIES™
Zoom Into the Zone			
Anchors Away!	10 minutes	Reproducible 13A, pencils or fine-line markers, small pieces of white paper (two inches by four inches), yarn or string (thirty-six inches) for each child	none
The Ruler Rules	5 minutes	none	gold shred, prism bag
BibleZone™			
Hot Rocks Rules	5 minutes	none	glitter balls
The Golden Rule	10 minutes	none	none
What's The Good Word?	15 minutes	Reproducible 13B, construction paper, glue, crayons or felt-tip markers, scissors	none
Heavenly Hopscotch	5 minutes	masking tape, Page 161	pom-poms
LifeZone			
Sing and Celebrate	5 minutes	cassette player	Cassette
Vortex Verse	5 minutes	none	none
If the Rule Fits	5 minutes	one yard yellow or gold ribbon	none

⊚ Zillies™ are found in the **BibleZone™ FUNspirational™ Kit.**

155

Zoom Into the Zone™

Choose one or more activities to catch your children's interest.

Supplies:
Reproducible 13A,
pencils or fine-
line markers,
small pieces of
white paper
(two inches by
four inches),
yarn or string
(thirty-six inches)
for each child

Zillies™:
none

Anchors Away!

(M)ake a copy of the puzzle code (*Reproducible 13A*) for each child in the group. Set out the supplies the children will need. (*Option: Cut pieces of white paper into three-inch by four-inch pieces. Cut a length of yarn about thirty-six inches long for each child.*)

Greet the children warmly as they come in. This is a good time to play the BibleZone™ theme song from the **Cassette**.

Say: In the puzzle there is a secret message written out in flags. Flags very similar to this are used on boats to send messages.

Option: Once the children have discovered the secret message in the puzzle (*Love one another as I have loved you*), let the children create secret messages for their friends. Use the pieces of white paper to make letter flags. Then hang the letter flags over the string or yarn. Hang somewhere in the room and let others read the messages.

Supplies:
none

Zillies™:
golden shred,
prism bag

The Ruler Rules

Gather the children in an open space. Make sure there is space to move without any child being in danger of injury.

Say: This is the perpetual motion kingdom. No matter what happens, you have to keep moving. (*Name of child***) is the ruler of the kingdom and will tell us how to move. (***Hand the child a piece of gold shred.***) You will continue to follow (***Name of child***) until I give someone else a piece of golden shred. Then that person becomes the ruler. The ruler can tell us to hop around the room. The ruler can tell us to skip around the room. The ruler can even tells us to crawl around the room. Whatever the ruler says is the law. This will continue until I run out of shred.**

Walk around the group eyeing each child carefully. Then select one child and hand him or her a piece of golden shred. Let that child tell the group how to move. Continue this movement until you hand a piece of shred to another child. Continue until each child in the group has been the ruler. Then bring the children together in the storytelling area.

Say: In this game our ruler had the gold. In our Bible story today, we hear about a golden rule. This rule will help us, too, know how to move. (*Collect the golden shred and put it back into the prism bag.***)**

Choose one or more activities to immerse your children in the Bible story.

Hot Rocks Rules

Supplies:
none

Zillies™:
glitter balls

Hand out the **glitter balls**, one to each child. There are different colors in the box: yellow, blue, clear, green, and red. Depending on the box, there are a variety of different combinations of numbers. Select one child to be IT.

Say: Every one of us has rules. Some are rules our families make for us. Some are rules the school makes for us. Some are rules the country or the state makes for us. Some are rules the Bible makes for us.

Ask: Why do you think we have rules? What do rules do for us? What do rules do for other people? Are there any rules that you think are unfair? Why?

Invite the children to think about the purpose behind rules. Share some of their feelings with the group.

Then say: We are going to play a game called HOT ROCKS. The HOT ROCKS are the glitter balls. We will begin to pass these balls around the circle. Everyone will have a ball. IT will stand facing away from the circle and at random call out HOT ROCKS! At that point everyone will freeze and hold onto the ball that is in her or his possession. IT will choose a color: red, blue, yellow, or green. The persons who are holding balls of that color will have to tell of a rule that he or she knows.

ZONE IN™ | **Jesus teaches us to treat others as we want to be treated.**

The Golden Rule

By Sharilyn S. Adair

At every hand popular culture is teaching your students to look out for Number One and to think first of his or her own pleasure. You could not teach them a more critical rule to guide their lives than the Golden Rule. Repetition will help them commit it to memory. Teach the children the following refrain to today's poem and have them say it several times until they are comfortable with the rhythm. Ask them to repeat it after every stanza that you recite. After reciting the poem, have the class discuss what they might do in each of the situations described if they followed the Golden Rule.

Jesus gave us a powerful rule
To help us be faithful and true:
In everything do to others as
you would have them do to you.

You're having great fun on the play-
    ground
with Bobby and Sally and Sue.
They say, "Tim's no fun. Let's ignore him."
So what are you going to do?

Jesus gave us a powerful rule
To help us be faithful and true:
In everything do to others as
you would have them do to you.

A video game that belongs to a friend
is one you would like to have too.
He lost it, and now you have found it.
So what are you going to do?

Jesus gave us a powerful rule
To help us be faithful and true:
In everything do to others as
you would have them do to you.

You're bored when you visit Aunt Lucy.
She talks till you think she'll turn blue.
But Mother says Aunt Lucy is lonely,
So what are you going to do?

Jesus gave us a powerful rule
To help us be faithful and true:
In everything do to others as
you would have them do to you.

Your brother feels bad, so he's grumpy
And takes out his anger on you.
He says that he's going to punch you,
so what are you going to do?

Jesus gave us a powerful rule
To help us be faithful and true:
In everything do to others as
you would have them do to you.

at home	at school
at church	at play
a friend's house	in the car
at ball practice	at the mall

Choose one or more activities to immerse your children in the Bible story.

Supplies:
Reproducible 13B, construction paper, glue, crayons or felt-tip markers, scissors

Zillies™:
none

What's the Good Word?

(M)ake a copy of the talking bear *(Reproducible 13B.)*

Say: In today's Bible lesson Jesus taught us to treat others as we want to be treated. Rather than wait for them to be nice to us, we should be nice to them first. Let's make talking cards with good words inside to send to friends.

Have the children cut out the bear card. Fold in half vertically with the bear's face on the outside. Make sure the diamond points formed by the dotted lines are on the fold. Then make a cut along the dark solid line (mouth of the bear). Stop where the solid line ends. It should be even on both sides. Open out flat and fold in reverse so that the bear face is on the inside. Then fold down the edges as shown here. Open the square. Push the mouth to the inside and fold in reverse along the other creases. Fold a sheet of construction paper in half. Then glue or tape the bear face inside the construction paper, matching the center fold lines. Make sure the mouth of the bear remains free.

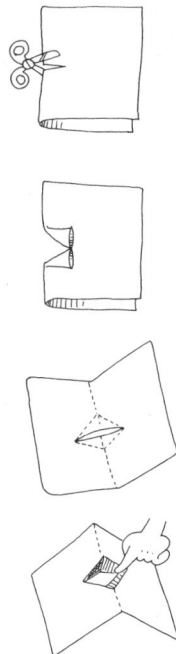

On the inside the children can write a message of encouragement or write the Bible verse to send to a friend. Remind the children that the Golden Rule is something that Christians should always follow every day.

Supplies:
masking tape, location cards (See page 161.)

Zillies™:
large pom-poms

Heavenly Hopscotch

(M)ake a copy of the location cards *(Page 161)*. Cut them apart. Lay out a hopscotch grid with eight spaces and a Heavenly Home space. Tape one of the location cards on each square. Use the traditional rules of hopscotch. Players will use the pom-pom as a marker and hop over the designed square. However, when a player retrieves his or her **pompom**, the player must contribute some act of kindness that can be performed in the location designated in that square.

Say: Remember, the Golden Rule doesn't just mean being kind to someone who is kind to you. It means treating someone else as you want to be treated, even if they don't treat you that way.

Choose one or more activities to bring the Bible to life.

Sing and Celebrate

Supplies:
cassette player

Zillies™:
Cassette

(M)ake a copy of the words for each child or create a class song chart. You may want to divide the group into two parts. Group 1 can sing the words in parenthesis and Group 2 can respond.

Be Nice

When someone is mean to you
there's only one thing you should do,
this is my advice
(What is it?) Be nice.
(Be nice?) Be nice, be nice, be nice.

REFRAIN:
'Cause it's nice to be nice
in all you do,
not just when someone's nice to you.
If somebody calls you names,
don't go out and do the same,
remember this advice:
(what is it?) Be nice.
(Be nice?)Be nice, be nice, be nice, be nice, be nice.

When somebody bursts your bubble,
better not start making trouble,
this is my advice
(What is it?) Be nice.
(Be nice?) Be nice, be nice, be nice.

Words: Janet McMahan-Wilson and Debra Black
© 1991 New Spring Publishing, Inc. (ASCAP), a division of Brentwood-Benson Music Publishing, Inc.
All rights reserved. Used by permission.
"Be Nice" from the Brentwood Music, Inc. recording *God's Way A Song A Day*, vol. 1

Life Zone ™

Choose one or more activities to bring the Bible to life.

Supplies:
none

Zillies™:
none

Vortex Verse

Have the children form a large circle holding hands.

Say: Repeat after me—Do to others as you would have them do to you.

Begin to chant the Bible verse as you move around in a circle. Then release your left hand and begin to coil inward, slowly leading the players on your right hand in a spiral inside the circle. Continue to say the Bible verse as you move in a circle. When you reach the center of the circle, turn around and begin to lead the players in a reverse spiral. Players following the incoming spiral will pass outgoing players walking in the opposite direction. To end, the entire group reforms into a circle and says the verse one last time together.

> **Jesus teaches us to treat others as we want to be treated.**

Supplies:
one yard yellow or gold ribbon

Zillies™:
none

If the Rule Fits

Tie a piece of yellow or gold ribbon into a loop that is big enough to fit over and around any child in your class. Have the children stand in a circle.

Say: I want you to think of something this week that you can do that will be an act of kindness you would want to be done to you. If the group agrees it'll fit the Golden Rule, then you slip on the loop, pass it down over your body, step out of it and hand it to the next person.

When everyone has had a chance to contribute something they can do in the coming week that will fit the Golden Rule, then have the children form a prayer circle.

Pray: Dear God, help us to treat one another as we want to be treated. Help us to follow the example that Jesus set for us. Amen.

Make a copy of HomeZone for each family in your class.

Bible Verse
Do to others as you would have them do to you.
Matthew 7:12

Bible Story
Matthew 7:12

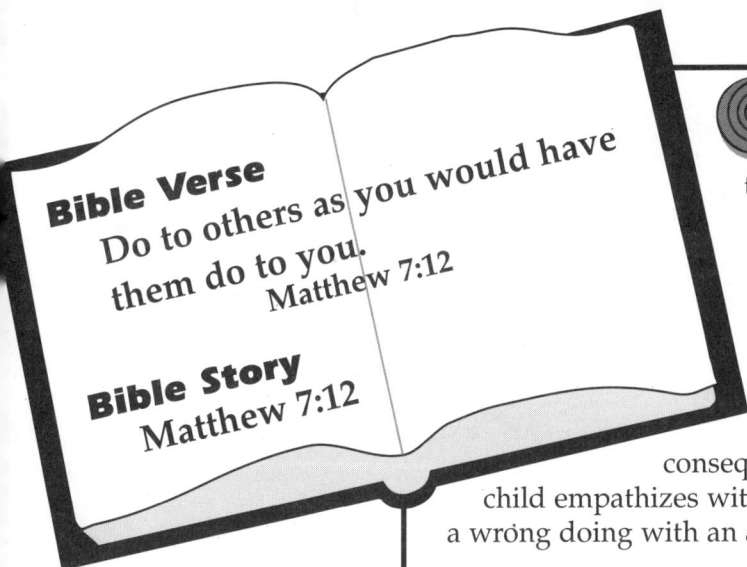

In today's Bible lesson your child heard the Scripture more commonly referred to as the Golden Rule. In this statement, J challenges followers to go beyond simply not doing wrong. As Christians, we are called to go the extra mile. The Golden Rule says to us that we should think about others and their happiness. Children know how they want to be treated and have probably experienced the consequences of bad behavior. Certainly your child empathizes with others, but may find it difficult to return a wrong doing with an action of love instead.

Make a Cross of Nails

You will need: one 2-inch nail and one 1 ½-inch nail, thin picture-hanging wire, purple or black yarn or cording, hammer

Blunt the ends of the nails by hammering the sharp end slightly. Lay the 1½-inch nail across the 2-inch nail, about one third of the distance from the nail head. Bind the nails together by tightly wrapping the wire around the two nails. Use a criss-cross technique. Then cover the wire in a similar technique. Attach a length of yarn or cording to wear the cross around your neck.

LifeZone
Lent is the forty days not counting Sundays prior to Easter. If this is the time when your child is participating in the Zone, then make a special effort to be involved in mission projects.

ZONE IN
Jesus teaches us to treat others as we want to be treated.

Anchors Away!

Reproducible 13A
Permission granted to photocopy for local church use. © 1998 Abingdon Press.

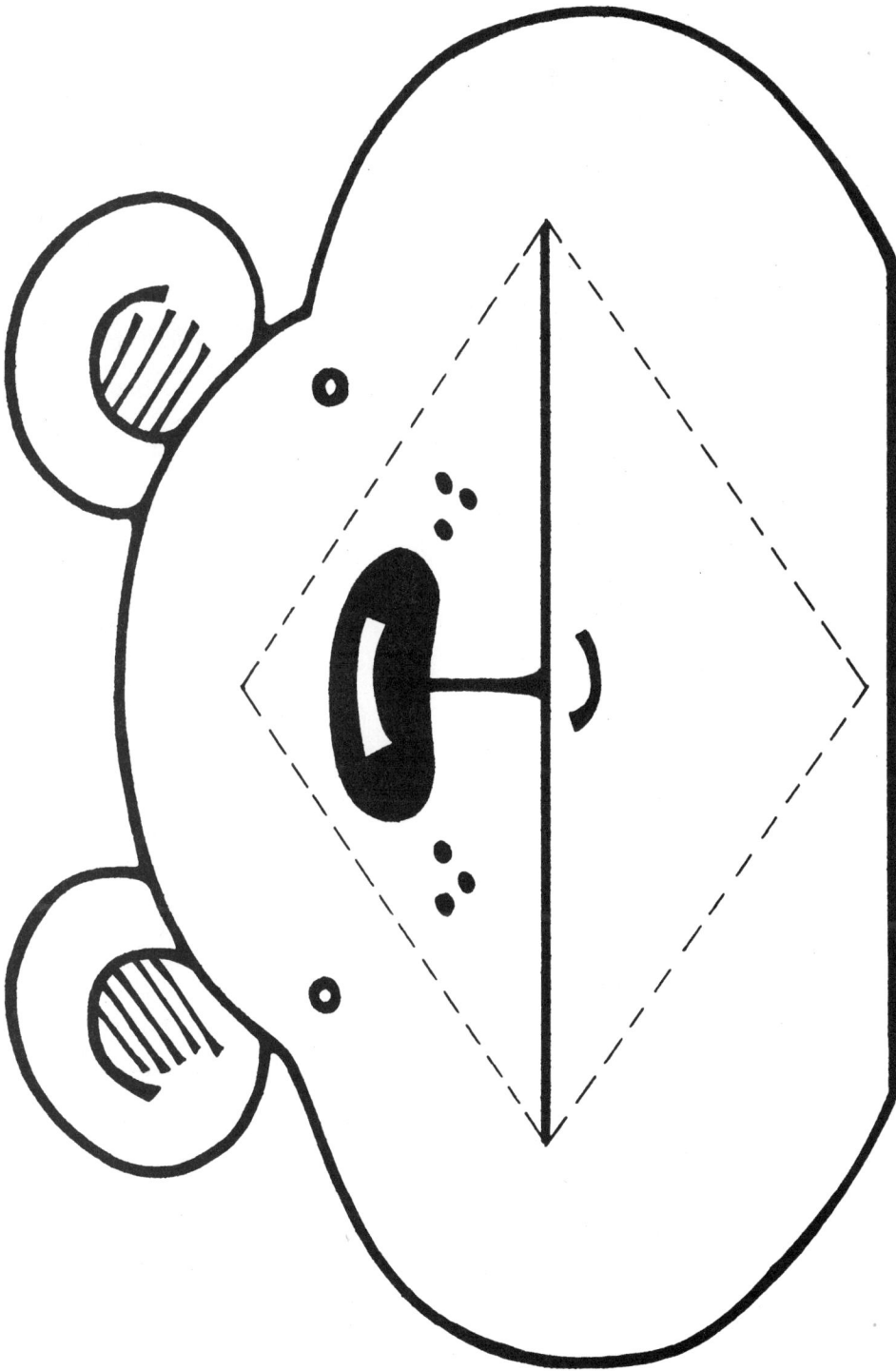

Reproducible 13B

Closet Chaos

Keep the activity level high with this action-packed relay.

Divide the children into equal teams. For each team create a pile of clothing. Include things such as: a bathrobe, an extra large tee-shirt, an adult-sized sweatshirt, adult-sized sweat pants, socks, a hat, mittens, earmuffs, a vest, and any other piece of clothing you may wish to use. Make sure each team has the same kinds of clothing.

The first runner on each team runs to the pile, puts everything on, then runs back to the next team member and helps him or her put on all the clothing. That team member runs back to the designated spot and removes the clothing and then runs back to his or her team. The next team member runs to the designated spot and puts all the clothing on. Continue until everyone has had a turn putting on all the clothing.

Nose to the Ground

Give each child a glitter ball. Create an obstacle course around the room on the floor. Use books, ramps, tunnels, and so forth.

Have the children negotiate their balls through the obstacle course using only their noses as propellants of the ball.

Human Tic-Tac-Toe

Players form two teams of five players each. Tape a matching piece of construction paper to the back of each child on a team, or devise some other means to designate commonality. Create a tic-tac-tow grid on the floor using masking tape. Teams must use group cooperative skills to play the game. The first team places a team member on the board. Then Team 2 places a member of its team on the grid. Continue until one team has three players in a row.

Mud Puddle Pie

Make your favorite brownie recipe in an 8-inch by 8-inch pan. Cut it into the shape of a mud puddle. Make a package of chocolate pudding. Spoon the pudding on top of the brownies, and poke gummy worms into the pudding.

Banana Fruit Fly

You will need: bananas, leafy lettuce, apples (thinly sliced), grapes, maraschino cherries, toothpicks.

Slice a small banana in half lengthwise. Place one half, flat side down, on a plate of leafy lettuce. Insert six apple slices (three on each side) into the banana. Make eyes by securing grapes to the banana with toothpicks. Cut a maraschino cherry into quarters; position one quarter to put a smile on the face.

Grand Slam-wich

Cut a piece of cardboard about twelve inches square. Cover with aluminum foil. Let the children make a favorite sandwich. Cut off the crusts, and cut the sandwich into four squares for the bases. (You might want an adult to supervise.)

Spread pieces of celery with peanut butter for the base paths. Place a grape "runner" on each base. For the pitcher's mound, use your favorite cookie.

Ready, Set, Create!

Younger elementary children enjoy expressing themselves creatively. But they often get frustrated with the end product. They want it to be perfect. Yet many of their fine motor skills are just beginning to develop. Cutting with scissors, drawing likenesses of objects, and coloring within the lines are all skills that will come through practice and maturity. Encourage art projects where the end result can be appreciated without having to be perfect or to look like everyone else's. Provide an atmosphere where experimentation with creativity is appreciated and even celebrated. You will be surprised at the results.

Kooky Covers

Schoolbooks don't have to look impersonal and boring. Give them a little *pizazz*! Cover them with your own personalized paper. Invite friends to work together and try several neat methods.

Batik Technique: Cut a brown paper grocery bag along one fold. Then cut off the bottom. Flatten the bag. With a thick crayon, color a heavy layer all over the bag (light, bright colors work best.) Crumple the bag, and place it in a bucket of water to create the crackle lines. Gently squeeze the bag, lay it flat, and let it dry. Brush dark watercolor paints over the crayon. Blot with paper towels if you need to. Then let the paint dry.

Swirly Paint Technique: Glob finger paint onto a sheet of construction paper. (The brighter the paint the better.) Use a comb, a paintbrush, a piece of cardboard with notches cut into it, or another tool to create patterns on the paper. Let the paint dry.

Song Zone™

Let the children listen to the song "The Bible Zone" from the Cassette as they enter the room or while working on lesson activities. Make copies of the words and let the children sing along.

The Bible Zone

Where else can we find a lesson learned on every page?
Stories that have lived to teach us all from age to age.
From the flood to parting waters, burning bushes,
        prophets, scholars,
God's Word takes us anywhere.

In the Bible zone where God's Word comes to life.
In the Bible zone our path is always bright.
A book for all creation to every boy and girl.
In the Bible zone is God's treasure for the world.

In the Bible zone where God's Word comes to life.
In the Bible zone our path is always bright.
A book for all creation to every boy and girl.
In the Bible zone is God's treasure for the world.

Learning of forgiveness or when learning how to pray,
God's Word gives examples of the things we face each day.
When we choose to look inside we see ahead or back in time.
God's Word takes us anywhere.

In the Bible zone where God's Word comes to life.
In the Bible zone our path is always bright.
A book for all creation to every boy and girl.
In the Bible zone is God's treasure for the world.

In the Bible zone where God's Word comes to life.
In the Bible zone our path is always bright.
A book for all creation to every boy and girl.
In the Bible zone is God's treasure for the world.

Words by David Hampton
© 1997 New Spring Publishing, Inc. (ASCAP), a div. of Brentwood-Benson Music, Inc.

Bible ONE

_____

Bible ONE

_____

Bible ONE

_____

Bible ONE

_____

Bible ONE

_____

Bible ONE

_____

Bible ONE

_____

Bible ONE

_____

WANTED

A SPECIAL CHILD OF GOD WHO WAS BORN TODAY!

HAPPY BIRTHDAY FROM YOUR FRIENDS IN THE ZONE

SHERIFF

To:

You're right on TARGET!

Good Work!

From:

Official Smile Award

Presented to

_____

For the Smile Category

_____

Presented by

_____

Date

Enter the Story Zone

Does the thought of telling a story to a group of children make your stomach do double back flips? Do the words "tell me a story" make you break out into a cold sweat? Then don't stop reading, this article is for you!

I am thoroughly convinced that inside every person is a storyteller just itching to get out. After all, we're all storytellers (with varying degrees of skill) at heart.

"But Bible stories are different!" you may whine. Not necessarily true. Telling a Bible story should be as easy as relating a story from your own childhood. The stories in the BibleZone™ are teacher-friendly and guaranteed to capture the interest of the children. After all, these stories come from a book we love and consider the foundation of our faith. Let's pass those stories on to the children so that the Bible can become THEIR book too.

So how do we start?

Step 1: Get familiar.
You can't tell it until you know it. That means reading it over and over and over again. Know the details of the story you are going to tell better than you know your name.

Step 2: Imagine the story.
Make a mental image of the story. Imagine what it would be like to be at the manger on the first Christmas. Imagine the cold, the smell of the animals. Once you have imagined the story, then the story becomes your own story.

Step 3: Consider the children.
Children are interested in action. What did the characters do? How did they feel? Let the story speak for itself. Ask important questions about the motives of the characters to help the children get underneath the story. But don't moralize. The children need to get the message for themselves.

Step 4: Practice, practice, practice.
Practice telling the story out loud. Watch your expression, your tone of voice, your body movements. Remember to speak clearly so that every child can hear and understand you. Be yourself, be natural, be relaxed.

Step 5: Involve the children.
Movement is an effective storytelling device. Children get involved in the story if their bodies are involved. Make sure the movements are well defined and easy to imitate. Practice these movements ahead of time. The stories in the Teacher's Guide often suggest movements. Use them.

Dress like one of the biblical characters and tell the story from that character's point of view. First person stories give opportunities for the storyteller to bring reality to the events in the story and to be dramatic. In fact, the children may well forget you are the teacher!

Even though **GREAT** storytellers are rare and should be national treasures, anyone can learn to be a **good** storyteller. The most important thing to remember is that you must love the stories and want to share them with the children. BibleZone™ is centered around favorite Bible stories. We want BibleZone™ to be the place where the Bible comes to life and where the children see the Bible as THEIR book, too.

It Worked for Us!

Sue Isbell from Knoxville, Tennessee sends this idea: We used BZ Bucks to reward the children for bringing their Bibles, bringing a friend, learning the Bible verse, and helping in the classroom. At the end of the quarter the children could trade their BZ Bucks in for stickers, pencils, erasers, or other small treasures. Thanks, Sue. Here are the bucks for those of you who want to try it.

Use the following scale to rate BibleZone™ resources
If you did not use a section, write "Did not use" in the Comments space.

1 = In No Lessons   2 = In Some Lessons   3 = In Most Lessons   4 = In All Lessons

1. *Enter the Zone* provided information that helped me teach this lesson's Scripture.

1   2   3   4   Comments:

2. The *Scope the Zone* chart made lesson planning easy.

1   2   3   4   Comments:

3. The teaching plan was organized in a way that made it easy to use.

1   2   3   4   Comments:

4. The Teacher's Guide provided easy-to-follow instructions for the learning activities.

1   2   3   4   Comments:

5. The supplies necessary to do the activities were easily located in my home or church.

1   2   3   4   Comments:

6. My students were able to understand the lesson's ZoneIn™.

1   2   3   4   Comments:

7. The activities matched the learning level and abilities of my students.

1   2   3   4   Comments:

8. The number of activities in the lesson plan worked for the time I had available (indicate how much time):_____.
   If not, check:_____ too many _____too few.

1   2   3   4   Comments:

9. I used activities from the GameZone™ section of the Teacher's Guide.

1   2   3   4   Comments:

10. I used activities from the ArtZone™ section of the Teacher's Guide.

1   2   3   4   Comments:

11. I used the Cassette in my classroom.

1   2   3   4   Comments:

12. I used items from the BibleZone™ FUNspirational™ Kit

1   2   3   4   Comments:

13. I sent the HomeZone™ page home to parents.

1   2   3   4   Comments:

14. Other stories I would like to see in BibleZone™ are:

ADDITIONAL COMMENTS

Activities my students enjoy the most are:

Activities my students enjoy the least are:

I use BibleZone™ for_____Sunday School _____Second Hour Sunday School _____Children's Church

_____Wednesday nights _____Sunday nights _____Children's Fellowship _____other

ABOUT MY CLASS

Number of Children at Each Age in My Class:

_____Age 6_____Age 7____Age 8

_____Other (Specify) _____

Average number of children who attend my class each week:_____

I teach: _____alone _____with another teacher each week

_____taking turns with other teachers _____with an adult helper

ABOUT MY CHURCH

_____Rural _____Small Town _____Downtown _____Suburban

_____Under 200 Members _____200-700 Members _____Over 700 Members

Church Name and Address:_____

_____

My Name and Address:_____

_____

Please return this form to   Susan Salley
Research Department
201 8th Ave., So
P.O. Box 801
Nashville, TN 37202-0801